UNLOCK THE SECRETS OF THE TAROT FOR A WONDERFUL SEX LIFE

Once you understand the sexual meaning behind the mysterious and beautiful symbols of the Tarot, you will be able to enhance your future love life. In the Tarot there is power to evoke thought that will help you make the romantic choices right for you.

THE SEXUAL KEY TO THE TAROT

❀   ❀

A Book for Lovers

Other SIGNET Mystic Books
You'll Want to Read

THE SEXUAL KEY
TO THE TAROT

THE LOVERS.

Theodor Laurence

A SIGNET BOOK

NEW AMERICAN LIBRARY

TIMES MIRROR

We should employ our passions in the service of life,
not spend life in the service of our passions.

RICHARD STEELE

Ⓢ SIGNET TRADEMARK REG. U.S. PAT. OFF. AND FOREIGN COUNTRIES
REGISTERED TRADEMARK—MARCA REGISTRADA
HECHO EN CHICAGO, U.S.A.

SIGNET, SIGNET CLASSICS, SIGNETTE, MENTOR AND PLUME BOOKS
are published by The New American Library, Inc.,
1301 Avenue of the Americas, New York, New York 10019

FIRST PRINTING, DECEMBER, 1973

1 2 3 4 5 6 7 8 9

PRINTED IN THE UNITED STATES OF AMERICA

Contents

Part Two
THE LESSER ARCANA
AND THEIR AUGURIES

Part Three
HOW TO MAKE A SPREAD

Part Four
CHOOSING AN AGENT

Introduction

The Tarot is a series of 78 playing cards decorated with symbol-pictures, of which 56 are the equivalents of ordinary playing cards plus four knights. The remaining 22 are pictorial keys, the symbolic nature of which is seen on their surface.

The four pre-eminent symbols of the Tarot are:

1. CUPS—corresponding to Hearts in the modern cards.

2. WANDS—corresponding to Diamonds in the modern cards.

3. SWORDS—corresponding to Spades in the modern cards.

4. PENTACLES (OR MONEY)—corresponding to Clubs in the modern cards.

In alternate Tarot descriptions Wands may be represented as Sceptres, Spears, or Lances; Pentacles as Coins or Money. For the sake of simplicity the four suits of Wands, Swords, Cups, and Money will be referred to throughout this work.

As it is with suit renditions, so it is with Tarot packs themselves, but again, for the sake of simplicity, let us confine our work to one suitable pack. In this case, that mystical Tarot pack developed by the British scholar Arthur Edward Waite which under his instruction was designed by his faithful co-worker, Pamela Colman Smith. This pack has become the most authoritative deck in existence, originally belonging to the Magical Order of the Golden Dawn. Mr. Waite was a profound student of magic, theosophy, occultism, alchemy, the Rosicrucians, the Holy Grail, the Kabbalah, and Freemasonry. Miss Smith was clairvoyant, of vivid imagination, and artistically competent. Together, Mr. Waite and Miss Smith have developed a most mystic and symbolic deck of Tarot cards which speak oracles to those "with ears to hear," and depict the gateway to truth for those "with eyes to see."

The art of fortune-telling (a term we use loosely) is one which has always enjoyed wide popularity. Volumes have been written on the subject and about the subject, and there are volumes yet to come, for with the dawning of this new Aquarian Age, mystical veils in every field of the occult are being lifted; unveiling not new and strange truths, but rather divulging greater depth and scope of truths which have been in existence as long as our universe itself. It is precisely the dawning of the Aquarian Age which brings this work to pass and makes it available to all men alike, and though this book bears the name of a man, he is in no wise the author of it but rather the channel through which the symbol-interpretation has flowed.

The Tarot, like Astrology, impels and does not compel. In the final analysis life is what we make it, but the Tarot can and does provide us with "measuring sticks," "arrows pointing the way," and "revelations of future events, causes, effects, and influences" which, when used wisely, may very well straighten our path of journey through this life. In short, forewarned is forearmed.

The neo-symbolism of this work, i.e. sexuality, is not new in the truest sense. Down through the ages great men and women have availed themselves of the sexual renderings of the Tarot but usually in mystical or secret orders. Bound by vows, sworn to secrecy, none have disclosed the Sexual Key to the Tarot. Being a fragment of Secret Tradition, the Sexual Key to the Tarot has not been heretofore publicized. The veil, as aforementioned, is being lifted and sexuality is coming to the fore, not being magnified but merely disclosed where it was earlier concealed, cloaked, suppressed, or sanctified.

It cannot be denied that even today men and women seek out fortune-tellers because they are in search of a mate, sexual satisfaction in life, or both. The three main reasons cards are consulted are Health, Wealth, and Sex, not necessarily in that order. The need deemed cogent by the Querent (he or she who seeks the wisdom of the cards) is that which causes him to gravitate to card-reading.

If you have ever known someone who has consulted a fortune-teller you may have noticed that though the Reader (fortune-teller) covered the spiritual, psychic, and material aspects of the Querent's present atmosphere (realm of life, aura) the Querent, whether male or female, was quite impressed by such statements from the Reader as, "There is a man (woman) in your life," "I see a dark-haired and passionate person in your immediate future," or "Happiness which you seek will come to you in the form of a warm, affectionate person." Usually the Querent is elated by such news. Why? Because the crux of the matter, their motivation, intent, and hope of the future is sexual fulfillment. Let us recognize maturely once and for all—there is nothing wrong in that. People want a full, satisfying life and we all have a divine right to exactly that. The Tarot often reveals the path of that promised life. Now, the "fullness of life" of which we speak is not totally sexual in nature, but since the Spiritual, Psychic, Mystic, and Supernatural aspects of the Tarot may be found in numerous other works, this book is dedicated to The Sexual Key to the Tarot.

Before we begin, there is one aspect of Tarot reading which cannot be written. That is, a card turned up during a reading indicates one of two persons—either the Querent, or someone in the Querent's life, whether past, present, or future, and as can be readily seen, this matter can only be resolved at an actual sitting with a qualified reader. In a self-reading, of course, the identification of each card will be ascertained by the individual reader.

THEODOR LAURENCE

Part One

THE MAJOR ARCANA, THEIR SEXUAL KEYS AND SIGNIFICATION

THE MAGICIAN.

I

The Magician

*The first card of the trumps major depicts
a youthful figure in the robe of a magician. . . .*

SEXUAL KEY   The magic of youth which, as a part of
a person's nature regardless of chronological age, manifests itself in youthful vigor and sexual adequacy, which
is objectified in smiles of confidence and shining eyes.

*. . . Above the magician's head is the sign of
life, the figure 8 in a horizontal position. . . .*

SEXUAL KEY   Life force, energy, and vitality, endless
and self-generative, is at the beck and call of the
Magician-nature.

*. . . about his waist is a serpent-cinture,
the snake appearing to devour its own tail. . . .*

SEXUAL KEY   Sexual self-love. The snake, always a
phallic-symbol, has hemipenes located in its tail and is
herein depicted in the act of self-fellation. In oral-genital
fashion the serpent, in a never-ending cycle, is alternately generating and fellating its own semen.

13

*... in the magician's right hand is another
phallic symbol, a wand, both ends of which
are pointed. ...*

SEXUAL KEY Sexual vitality is centrally located and
issues forth from that psychical central point, or realm.
The Magician's hands grip the middle of the phallic
symbol, the source of all sexual energy. His hand
divides the wand into two equal parts, one pointing
heavenward, the other earthward, signifying sexual
balance and also sexual opposites.

*... On the table in front of the magician
are the symbols of the four Tarot suits,
signifying on the one hand the elements of
natural life: The wand indicates the fire
signs* (depicting Lust, Anger, and Passion); *
the cup indicates the water signs* (depicting
Urine, Blood, and Semen); *the sword, the
earth signs* (depicting Flesh, Force, and
Malleability); *and the pentacles, the air
signs* (depicting Flatus, Eructation, and
Respiration). *On the other hand the four
Tarot suits signify the elements of social
life: The wand indicates power; the cup indicates intoxicants* (often concomitant with
sexual activity); *the sword indicates aggression;
and the pentacle indicates money.*

SEXUAL KEY All the elements represented and implied
by the symbols of the four suits are at the disposal of
the Magician, to be drawn upon and utilized at will,
rendering members of the opposite sex of all Zodiacal
signs (Fire, Water, Earth, Air) worthy game for sexual
pursuits.

SEXUAL SIGNIFICATION
OF THE MAGICIAN CARD

A person with the Magician-nature possesses the magic of youth, demonstrating youthful vigor in both sexual pursuit and sexual activity. He may be disposed to pedophiliac impulses, seeking to unite his or her own psychic youth with a child exhibiting comparable physical youth. The strength, vitality, and sexual endurance of the young does not pose problems of sexual incompatability for the Magician-nature, for no matter what its chronological age, it recognizes the endless flow of sexual energy signified by the horizontal 8, which this nature may call upon at any time. However, when this ready accessibility of sexual energy is misconstrued as abiding within the human organism, the Magician-nature exhibits self-love. Thus enamored of his or her "own" sexuality, masturbatory practices are frequently and secretly perpetrated, and such a nature would, were it possible, commit a solitary oral-genital manipulation as represented by the self-fellating serpent. The well-oriented individual whose nature corresponds with that of the Magician enjoys a life of sexual balance, although his methodology may be misunderstood by the masses. As indicated in the two-headed phallic symbol, the wand, this nature may fluctuate between periods of celibacy and periods of hypersexuality. This nature's periods of celibacy are often accompanied by feelings of guilt, its periods of hypersexuality accompanied by empirical disregard for existing mores. During the latter, all members of the opposite sex are totally appealing to this nature which, under the harmonious circumstances, can adjust itself to any personality trait or personality flaw because it is not the means which is important but the end—the love object. In yet another sexual being the two-headed phallic symbol, the wand, takes on different connotations—bisexuality. This Magician-nature (and only individual Querents know who they are) can enjoy sexual activities with either sex with equanimity.

In a spread (a reading) this card means: Querent struggling to control sexual destiny; will power over opposite sex; trickery and guile in obtaining sex partners. It also means skill and diplomacy used to obtain sexual gratification, qualities made effective by confidence and will, attributes of the Magician-nature. For a female, in addition to the foregoing, this card indicates "magical sexual powers" which may lie in her ability to create a pleasant sexual atmosphere for and with the love object of her choice.

THE HIGH PRIESTESS

II

The High Priestess

*She has the lunar cresent at her feet. It
is not yellow in color as in the floor, but
grey, signifying the grey matter of flesh. . . .*

SEXUAL KEY The vagina, ever yawning during that
period of receptivity in its never-ending increscence
from unsated to sated, here depicted in its unsated
cycle, signifying lack and need, but relegated to a lower
position (at her feet), sensual and sexual use of the
vagina of secondary utility.

*Upon her head a crown comprising a globe
flanked by horns. . . .*

SEXUAL KEY Upper, over, foremost, primary, above
all. Hence, the crown. The globe, also grey in color and
symbolizing flesh, signifies completeness of fleshy pursuits, fullness of fleshly appetites, a state of carnal
satiation. The High Priestess-nature knows all concerning sexuality and its myriad of uses. In this respect she
represents the "dream girl," the "perfect woman." The

globe, because it is fleshly grey and because it is a full, completed circle, also symbolizes the vagina but now in its sated form (the opposite of the lunar crescent). The geographical location of the two symbols (the lunar crescent, the globe) indicates the sexual outlook of the High Priestess-nature; a vagina should be full and sated, never or rarely empty and hungry. Geographically symbolized, sexual gratification is "up," sexual frustration is "down." That the globe is sided by two horns (phallic symbols) indicates her mental awareness of the needs of male phalli. It is this penile awareness which makes her the "perfect woman," she who is cognizant of all the sexual facts of life, "a girl after one's own heart." She exists in all women once they recognize their true sexual role in a man's life.

. . . On her breast is a large solar cross. . . .

SEXUAL KEY   This emblem symbolizes the sanctification of the "heart," from whence comes her uninhibited sexual expression and free spirit in her sexuality with men of her choice; where "sin" does not exist. In love she will utilize her sexual knowledge, ardent passion, and her vagina consecutively or simultaneously with "all her heart," and the man in her life will know complete and gratifying sexual ecstasy.

. . . In her hands, inscribed with the word
"TORA," is a scroll partly covered by her
robe. . . .

SEXUAL KEY   That the scroll is partly concealed implies that her sexuality is only partly objectified. The complete woman is not evident simply because she induces sexual pleasure. The scroll (phallus), half-hidden, signifies that a man who is true to her, who has won her "heart," will find in her, via the path of her objectified free and open sexuality, deeper and unforeseen delights.

As for the word "Tora," this and the word "penis"

each vibrate, numerologically, to 9, the mystical number denoting completeness, fulfillment.

... She is seated between two pillars,
one dark and one light. ...

SEXUAL KEY   The symbolization is threefold. One, like the half-hidden scroll, the dark and light pillars (phalli) represent the secret and the obvious respectively, the two aspects of her total sexuality. Two, as symbols of erected, sexually-charged phalli, the two pillars signify her acceptance of man and his penis without discrimination, yet another indication of her free spirit in sexual matters. Three, the bloomed, flowering heads of the pillar-phalli are portents. They symbolize her promise of eruptive and violent orgasms for men with whom she cohabits.

... Her vestments are flowing and gauzy. ...

SEXUAL KEY   These represent continuity of sexual expression.

... And her mantle is blue. ...

SEXUAL KEY   Signifying radiant emanation of mind, spirit, and body, each of which or all of which insure sexual fulfillment.

SEXUAL SIGNIFICATION
OF THE HIGH PRIESTESS CARD

In a reading this card represents the Querent (if female or homosexual) or someone in the Querent's life (a female or a homosexual), signifying the perfect woman all men dream about and long for, the woman who can satisfy their sexual desires far beyond their wildest thoughts. She intuitively knows the value to a man of a loving and sexually expressive female who can gratify him. She is the spirit of motherhood and is associated with the earth from which all things flow. A woman of the High Priestess-nature will please a man in every way she can, barring no sexual activity. In the case of unesthetic men lacking higher ideals, men motivated by infantile or primitive sexuality, a woman of this nature will artfully exploit the sexual field and since "sin" does not exist for her where love is concerned she will take active and exuberant part in any sexual act pleasing to her man. The High-Priestess-nature does not recognize the term "sexual perversion."

In a spread this card means: Passion, moral or physical ardor; secrets; the future of sexual union as yet unrevealed; safety from pregnancy and venereal disease; strength of sexual knowledge triumphs over evil influences. A man finding this card in his spread has this type of woman in his life and she will give him all her sexual strength to cope with life's problems. If he is a libidinal lamb she will make him a licentious lion. In a woman's spread the Querent will realize these qualities within herself and will feel she has found her ultimate reason for living. Those of latent homosexuality, male or female, finding this card in a spread may very well expect a person of marked concupiscence to enter their realm of existence.

THE EMPRESS.

III

The Empress

*The third card of the Trumps Major presents
a stately figure having rich garb
and royal bearing. . . .*

SEXUAL KEY   Typifies the initiator of sexual partnerships, the leader in such partnerships, and the mother
of sexual invention during such partnerships.

. . . Her crown is a cluster of twelve stars. . . .

SEXUAL KEY   Twelve is the mystical number of government, here meaning she governs sexual matters, and
because they are stars, her government is shining and
radiant. The acini-form of the stars, like that of grapes,
symbolizes sexual fruitfulness, an abundance of succu-
lent delights.

*. . . On the heart-shaped shield beside her
is the symbol of Venus. . . .*

SEXUAL KEY   At fingertip reach is her passion, her
fertile sexuality, her vibrant sexual organs, comely and

hypersensitive, to be used at will as a shield against cold-hearted men, impotent men, bestial men—her Venusian capabilities rendering all men docile and lovable.

... There is a waterfall beyond her and in front of her a field of ripening corn. ...

SEXUAL KEY   The water denotes her stream of vaginal fluids, as limitless as mountain streams. The waterfall depicts power and represents the ferocity and power of her orgasms. The field of ripening corn is the symbol of her fertility and the ripening fruit of her sensual body.

... The globe of this world surmounts her sceptre. ...

SEXUAL KEY   Clearly a phallic symbol, the sceptre is held gingerly by the Empress, denoting her high regard for, and fearlessness of, the male penis. She holds the sceptre aloft as though to exalt it as she does in her life. The proximity of the symbol to her face suggests her propensity for fellatio, and is further suggested by the enlarged and bulbous head of the symbol, representing the male penis at the point of orgasmic ejaculation, having reached such a state by her impassioned and devoted fellating. That the head is globular secondarily suggests her pursuit of worldly pleasures and its green color denotes the fruitfulness of her sexual pursuits.

... She is pictured full-faced. ...

SEXUAL KEY   Symbolized here is openness of character, frankness and candor in sexual matters, and sexual engagement with utter abandon. The Empress-nature conceals nothing, gives all, and greatly enjoys her sexual expression as much as the male who gleans her sensual fruit. The card signifies the gate needed to gain entry into the Garden of Venus, the secret of which is known to the Empress. The way which leads out is the secret known to the High Priestess.

SEXUAL SIGNIFICATION OF THE EMPRESS CARD

A woman (or homosexual) of the Empress-nature chooses her sexual mates and cannot be coerced, cajoled, bought, or trapped into sexual expression. She is the instigator of fleshly endeavors, having authority over her own passions, but once a male sex partner has been chosen, he shall know paradisiacal sensual pleasure at her hands as her passions come into play. The Empress-nature is worldly and loves sex. She enjoys sexual relations with such relish that when inspired to lust, she invents variations on the sexual theme which afford her and her loved one a harvest of orgasmic fruit. She is an ideal sex partner who enjoys intercourse often and her every sexual act is radiant with such orgiastic abandon that even her orgasms are electric, her released vaginal fluids abundant. Her hypersexuality is always signified by moist vaginal labia, a symbol she bears with pride, her personal sign of complete womanhood. The Empress-nature is the door to sexual pleasure. She adores the male organ, esteems it as the only worthy organ and will worship it openly and without shame, like a religious devotee worshipping at an altar. Her esteem manifests itself in overt sexual acts such as fellatio and scrotolingus. She will kiss, tongue, and mouth the male genitals with the same dedication she devotes to copulation. Whatever the sexual act, she gives her all.

In a spread this card denotes: Fruitfulness, action, and initiative in, for, and about sexual expression. It predicts fertility and good luck for those who wish

many orgasms. It is a card assuring a rich harvest of
sexual pleasure and dynamic orgasms as a reward for
the physical labor and sensual toil of courtship, foreplay, and intercourse.

THE EMPEROR.

IV

The Emperor

*In his right hand he holds his sceptre
and in his left hand a red globe. . . .*

SEXUAL KEY The sceptre as usual is a phallic symbol
but herein takes on a greater degree of meaning, the
representation illustrating an elongated and erect penis,
longer than normal, indicating mastery. The symbol is
a phallus at the precise point of vaginal penetration, the
crossbar symbolizing the labia majora, and the crowning
circle emblemizing the vaginal canal, open for willing
penetration. The red globe represents (*One*) worldly
pursuits and raw animal passion, which qualifies the
further symbolization of (*Two*) a sated vagina (as with
the globe upon the head of the High Priestess). That
the globe is red in color typifies the fires of passion, the
heat of lust, and the blood-red flush of a raging vagina
inflamed by penile friction of the vulva canal. The
red color, under proper circumstances, also further
depicts the blood of defloration.

He is a crowned Emperor. He is command-
ing and stately. The arms of the throne on
which he sits are fronted by rams' heads. . . .

SEXUAL KEY   The crown, of course, bespeaks mastery
over all. The gems inlaid thereon are five in number,
five being the mystical number signifying a nature quick,
witty, ingenious, intelligent, scientific, changeable, per-
suasive, and enterprising; qualities the Emperor employs
adroitly to capture the hearts of those females he wishes
to sexually possess. Homoerotically, the qualities are
expertly used to capture the hearts of the members of
the same sex. The rams' heads mark the Emperor's
sexual mastery, capabilities, aggressiveness, and prowess, the ram always used in ancient fertility rites because
of its huge phallus. That there are two heads designates
the dual desiderata of the Emperor's replete phallus—
strength and size.

He is the power of this world, clothed
in its highest natural attributes. He is
the virile power to which the Empress re-
sponds . . .

SEXUAL KEY   The ultimate in masculinitiy, sexual
dominance, and source of sensual pleasure for females.
Homosexually, the ultimate in sodomitic endeavors.
In this sense it is he who seeks to rupture the Hymen of
Woman, yet she remains *virgo intacta,* notwithstanding
the Emperor's profligate endeavors to fornicate all
women. The young males appealing to the masterful
homosexual also remain heterosexual despite the Emperor's homoerotic advances.

SEXUAL SIGNIFICATION
OF THE EMPEROR CARD

The Emperor-nature is the male counterpart of the Empress-nature. When sexually inverted the Emperor-nature is found in women and manifests itself as Lesbian sexuality and the Empress-nature is found in males and manifests itself as homosexuality. Though the state is often implied it should be understood that the condition of married life is not necessarily represented by this card and the card of the Empress. The Emperor-nature is autonomous and is as worldly and in love with sex as is the Empress-nature. The Emperor-nature, too, when inspired to lust, invents variations of the sexual acts which afford him and his loved ones a harvest of orgasmic fruit. His proclivity for coitus borders on the satyrical, which is pleasing to the females in his life. They are smitten of his sexual technique, his utter worship of female genitalia, which is the source of repetitive sexual joy for them. Women are sensuously ecstatic by the endurance of his penile erection and his fantastically profuse ejaculatory capacity, not to mention his uncanny copulative ability.

In a spread this card foretells sexual power and stability; also authority and will in sexual affairs. It suggests sexual mastery resulting in the dominance over and satiation of female sexual organs and libidinal demands. This is the card of the masterful lover, the libertine of ultimate passions, the idol of sexually frustrated women, and the "dream man" of young searching virgins.

THE HIEROPHANT

V

The Hierophant

The triple crown is upon his head, the
sceptre in his left hand terminates in
the triple cross, and there are three
crosses on his vestment. . . .

SEXUAL KEY   Three is the divine number of trinity, popularly used to represent God, Father, Son, and Holy Spirit; and man, mind, body, and spirit. The Hierophant is spirituality and religion who denies, minimizes, obviates, and retreats from sexuality. The sceptre phallic symbol is in his left hand, designating the Hierophant's negative attitude toward the penis and its sexual function. Sex, then, is to the left, and "not right." The phallic symbol, rather than bearing a bulbous head, bears three crossbars, the third and highest being shorter than the previous two. Mystically, the three crossbars imply that beyond the labia majora of the female genitals (sex for sex's sake), and beyond psychic and emotional relationships (sex for love's sake), there is a

28

third goal greatly to be desired; a goal absent of sensuality, opposed to fleshly appetites, devoid of orgasmic pleasure; a goal which promises a sexual ecstasy, sterile bliss, and elevated union. The succession of the three crossbars further implies that the third level is reached by those who have experienced the first two. The three crosses upon the Hierophant's vestment signify purity—a cross over the heart, a cross over the solar plexis (the seat of emotions), and a cross over the phallus and genitals, sanctifying each.

. . . He is seated between two pillars. His right hand is raised in benediction. . . .

SEXUAL KEY   The pillars are not those of the High Priestess, symbolic of highly desirable phalli. The columns of the Hierophant, though in the emblematic state of ejaculation, are grey and black in color, dark in form, and, despite the obvious symbolism of their ferocity and virility, they are relegated to the rear and to the sides, suggesting they exist only on the periphery of true reality. While the Hierophant's right hand is raised in blessing, it is a blessing bestowed upon those away from sexuality. His hand points back at the phalli in a gesture condemnatory of sexuality and sensuality and bodily pleasure. The phallic symbols then receive the back of his blessing, the reverse of his blessing, i.e. a curse.

. . . At his feet are the crossed keys. Before him kneel two devotees. . . .

SEXUAL KEY   The two keys unlock the gates of heaven and hell, and because the Hierophant has them, he ostensibly possesses the power to use them. The two devotees, both male, represent the subjugation of "maleness" or masculinity in the Hierophant-nature. That there are two repeats the symbolism of the first two crossbars of the Hierophant's sceptre. These two (sex

for sex's sake and sex for love's sake) desire to humble
themselves before God in order to gain inner peace.
They fail to recognize, however, that they are humbling
themselves before doctrine, religion, tradition, and
head of it all, the Hierophant, who, in the final analysis,
is a man like unto themselves.

SEXUAL SIGNIFICATION
OF THE HIEROPHANT CARD

The Hierophant-nature runs from sex in all its
aspects, treating even thoughts of sex as sin. This nature
is superstitious, fearful, and full of doubt. It is ignorant
of the purpose of its own virility or muliebrity. Penile
erections in the male and clitoral excitation in the
female keep this nature in a constant state of dread of
its own sexuality. Because of this nature's fear of open
and natural sexual relations, masturbatory practices are
frequently perpetrated and these are usually followed by
haunting and debilitating feelings of guilt.

Devoted servitude to mankind is manifested by this
nature, the natural but sublimated sex instinct re-
canalized. The Hierophant-nature excels in occupations
of service and makes excellent clergy. Married men of
this nature engage in sexual intercourse only infre-
quently and then as a matter of conjugal duty. During
the actual sex act these natures will strive, not for complete gratifying orgasm, but for minimal pleasure.

A male of this nature is subservient to women, passive in love-making, and prefers the female to take the
upper position in coitus, which allows him to divorce
himself from his erected penis, leaving the woman to
her own "sinful" devices. If the Hierophant-nature
emerges from his cocoon of sexual fear unboldly, he
first manifests lack of confidence in his own mascu-

linitiy. He overcompensates by cowering, bowing, scraping, coddling, and catering to women. He becomes adept at cunnilingus, practically an expert at oralism, a compensatory art developed in hopes that demands upon his awkward and reluctant penis will be minimal. When the Hierophant-nature yields naively to the pull of his flesh, he overdoes it, and takes on the characteristics of a pervert, a sexual misfit, or, in the modern vernacular, "a dirty old man." The sexual technique of oralism which he perpetrates to convince himself of his virility appears depraved and anaphrodisiac. He therefore attracts females of like characteristics and hence finds himself in a worse state of sexuality than before. Because of his or her proclivities, the Hierophant-nature can be easily abused sexually, and usually is. This is the basis for this nature's assertion that he has been to heaven and hell.

In a spread this card means: Alliance, captivity, servitude, overkindness, weakness, superstition, doubt. Such attributes, though conducive to success in occupations of service, suggest lack of confidence in one's own masculinity or femininity. In cases where a female doubts her own femininity and consequently prefers, desires, and enjoys oral-genital practices which afford her gratifying orgasms, the perfect sexual partner is the Hierophant-nature. This card further means homosexuality, latent or overt. It is the position of the card in relation to other modifying cards which gives its ultimate rendering, but generally speaking, it is the homosexual card. Because of the card's esoteric symbolism denoting a nature's deliberate escape from one's own sexuality, a male of this nature, abhorring the masculine role of his phallus, may turn to sodomy, playing the passive role. In a female of this nature, her abhorrence of fearful penes may turn her to lesbianism, having preference for the softness and gentleness of female mouths.

THE LOVERS.

VI

The Lovers

Above a great winged figure with arms extended, the sun shines in the zenith. . . .

SEXUAL KEY   The sun always represents consciousness —direct light rather than reflected light—but the brown color of the sun herein indicates lack of radiance, consciousness dimmed. The serenity of the winged creature, hands open and gentle in benediction, signifies all is well upon the earth, and "all," in this higher sense, means exactly that. Everything under the sun, that is, is good.

. . . In the foreground are a naked man and a naked woman, as if Adam and Eve in Paradise. The tree of life, bearing twelve fruits, is behind the man. Behind the woman, the serpent is twining around the tree of knowledge of good and evil. . .

SEXUAL KEY   The nakedness of the individuals, openly exhibiting their genitalia, symbolizes virginity, innocence, and love before it is contaminated by knowledge of gross sexual desire. Virginity herein does not mean that the man and woman have never copulated, but rather that in their sexual expression there exists no sin, disgrace, or shame. These negative elements do not exist until man eats of the fruit of the Tree of Knowledge of Good and Evil, that is, until man consciously accepts such elements as real and identifies with them. The message is: "As you believe, so you are." The card itself intimates the great mystery of Womanhood, more a working of a Secret Law of Providence than a mere manipulation by a willing and conscious seductress. This Secret Law suggests that it is through Woman's imputed lapse that Man shall arise ultimately. This is the card of sexual freedom, and, in a higher sense, it suggests that only by Woman can Man complete himself.

SEXUAL SIGNIFICATION
OF THE LOVERS' CARD

Men and women of the Lovers' nature do not believe in or adhere to traditional, hand-me-down, sexual taboos. When such natures are in love, they love openly and without shame, giving their sexual partner all they have. They will actively share in any sex act without reservation for they do not recognize "sex for love's sake" as sinful, disgraceful, or shameful. They have not eaten of the Tree of Knowledge of Good and Evil, and therefore continue to enjoy the virginal and innocent sexual expression of paradise—which is a state of mind. The Lovers'-nature intuitively knows the Secret Laws of Providence, which, in essence, is: "God created sexual union, the ultimate results of which are justifiably mystical, symbolic, and presently beyond human understanding." That which was mystical and which is now unveiled is this: In nature, the closest thing to the ideal mystical trance is the point of orgasm. The color of the sun is significant herein for it indicates sensuality, sexuality, and human love, as developmental stages which may lead one to integration and the fullness of life.

In a spread this card means: Unadulterated love; attraction; beauty; trials overcome; sexual union, sometimes marriage. It may predict "the other woman" in a man's life; "the other man" in a woman's life. Herein is the desire for virginal love; that is, strong fluid love with uninhibited sexual expression. The message of the Lovers is "Love conquers all," and "perfect love casteth out all fear."

THE CHARIOT.

VII

The Chariot

The victorious hero, erect and princely,
carries a drawn sword. He triumphantly
rides in his oncoming chariot bearing a
star-studded canopy of blue which is drawn
by two sphinxes, one dark, one light. In
the background are many red-roofed buildings
and a flowing river.

SEXUAL KEY His stature signifies great confidence in his masculinity; confidence borne of fulfilling and proficent sexual demonstrations. The star-studded blue canopy signifies royal vestment but he wears none on his person. Unlike the Emperor who inherits rulership regardless of merit, and the Hierophant who graduates to leadership by dint of seniority, the Charioteer earns his kingship by virtue of sexual excellence and indomitable sensuality. Therefore, he is more a king than he who possessses hereditary or unearned royalty. The sphinx indentifies with conquest and on this account, two pull his chariot. The color of the sphinxes has

35

further symbolism, typifying the degree of sensuality of the females he has conquered and will conquer in the future, ranging from the meek and demure female (dark), to the precocious and demonstrative female (light); from the sexually retiring female to the sexually puissant female.

In the background are many red-tipped buildings, some taller than others, all phallic symbols, and yet all represent one phallus, that of the Charioteer. The variegated height and breath of the structures denote the many conditions of penile erection demonstrated by the conqueror, suggesting uncanny sexual adjustment to many different female tastes and conditions. Notwithstanding his adaptability, the structures are red-tipped, signifying complete and impassioned orgasms with every female in his past. The diamond-tipped phallic symbol in his right hand promises similar orgasms with females yet in his future.

The blue wings and brown circle on the face of his chariot symbolize his readiness to fly to the next female orifice, be it oral, vaginal, or anal. The bright red coupling depicted just below the wings and circle represents the erect clitoris within the cincture of an inflamed vagina. That the females in the Charioteer's life realize sexual satiation is symbolized by the great wide river, a continuous and rampant flow of vaginal excretions.

SEXUAL SIGNIFICATION
OF THE CHARIOT CARD

The Charioteer-nature wins the heart and body of any female who excites his libidinal intrests. He is a conqueror of women, but also the conqueror of barriers between him and the sexual object of his choice. This quality, plus that of being a king by conquest rather

than heredity, makes even housewives fair game for
him. He makes cuckolds of kings; that is, husbands who
are kings in their own right in that a man's home is his
castle. When the Charioteer-nature casts his sensual
eye upon the wife of another man, nothing can stop
him from sexually possessing her, for no matter where
her reservations lie, he conquers them for her. The
female therefore realizes a freedom foreign to her and
enjoys complete sexual abandon with him even though
she at once knows she cannot possess him for her own.
He, and the orgiastic pleasures, will always be sweet
memories to her in her world with the "king" by marriage. The Charioteer-nature has no time for sweet
memories and rampages headlong into yet another
sexual affair with another female.

In a reading this card means: progress with females;
good news of forthcoming sexuality; conquest of barriers
to orgasm. It tells of triumph over enemies, obstacles,
and delays. It suggests victory in sexual pursuits through
the hard work of convincing females that sexual intercourse is good for them. If the person questioning the
cards is sexually frustrated, gratification and orgasm
are indicated. This card in a female's spread means
she will meet a man of this nature.

VIII

Strength

A woman, over whose head is a horizontal 8,
the sign of infinity, is closing the jaws of
a red lion which is being led by a chain of
flowers. In the background, a purple mountain.

SEXUAL KEY The horizontal 8 indicates the creativity of Woman, which is endless. The red lion represents the fiery passion and burning lust of man. That the woman is closing the lion's mouth with her bare hands indicates that man is willing to have his passions tamed by Woman. The secret of her strength lies in the chain of flowers, each flower representing an orgasm. The chain, therefore, is a series of dynamic and pleasurable orgasms linked together by her insatiable lust. The presence of the chain presupposes much sexual pleasure, frequent oral-genital play, and consummate coition.

SEXUAL SIGNIFICATION
OF THE STRENGTH CARD

Woman's creativity is manifested by her atavistic demonstration of feminine wiles and coital use of her genitalia to create a life of happiness and sexual bliss. A woman of this nature is a danger to the Charioteer-nature, or to any man enjoying sexual freedom, for she possesses the means to sate his every sexual appetite. If a man be her choice of a mate, she will and can go to any sexual lengths to tame him. This nature knows the man of her choice has already enjoyed various sex acts with various simpler women, so she, broadminded and hyper-sexual, incorporates all sex acts, perpetrating each with agile precocity, dazzling her lover into submission. That she can and will satisfy the most voracious penis is symbolized by the purple mountain behind her.

In a spread this card means: Sexual power and energy; coital activity and creativity; courage in the face of competition; generous exhibition and utilization of the sexual organs; complete success in the pursuit of genitalia. It denotes willpower in affairs of the heart, and a winning attitude of mind and body over matter and obstacle. A man finding this card in his reading will have such a female in his life. A woman finding it in her reading is being told that she has the sexual strength, coital ability, and feminine wherewithal to overcome the obstacles separating her from the man she desires at the moment.

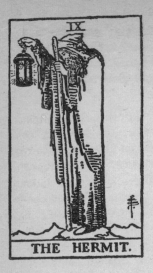

THE HERMIT.

IX

The Hermit

*The Hermit is seen on a white eminence, hold-
ing up his beacon. In his left hand is his
staff, and his bowed head is topped with a
cap of blue. The backdrop is also blue.*

SEXUAL KEY   Blue always signifies attainment. The
Hermit lives in a world of attainment. He is not a seeker.
He is not lost. Some have rendered the meaning of this
card as such but they are in error. The Hermit has
found what men seek. He has arrived. He is home. He
is a knower. The light he carries is not used to find his
own way. He stands upon a high place above the world.
The light is for those who follow, that they may see
where they are going. The Hermit's message is: That
where I am, ye may also be. The staff, a phallic symbol,
in his left hand does not relegate sexuality to obliv-
ion as in the case of the Hierophant, but rather signifies
that sexuality, once mastered, need no longer occupy a
place of supreme importance.

SEXUAL SIGNIFICATION
OF THE HERMIT CARD

The Hermit-nature, like the Charioteer, has attained sexual excellence, but not by conquest. Here is a lover of the ninth order who has tasted as much of sexual experience as the ferocious Charioteer, but whereas the latter is demanding and mercurial in his sexual relations, the Hermit-nature is the gourmet who has given countless females sexual gratification. The Charioteer may bring a female to violent orgasm but the Hermit is capable of producing and maintaining a steady, even flux of orgasmic bliss in a female. The one gains merely sexual gratification, no matter how many women he fornicates, whereas the Hermit, gaining sexual satisfaction in process, also gains knowledge of female desires and insight into their sexual motivations and needs—the secret of his complacency.

The blue of his cap, which covers his mind symbolically, denotes the sexual knowledge which he possesses and applies effectively. The Hermit-nature need not brandish a conquering sword (the dominating penis), but may proceed through life secure in the knowledge of female needs and desires. He is content with the act that he can readily supply what women want, and more. Though his head is bowed, take note that his shoulders do not sag as though in dejection and his back is not bent as though in defeat. The Hermit-nature is more than he appears to be. Beneath his cloak of humility is hidden the body of a one-hundred-percent man. Masculinity and sexual prowess are at his beck and call, beneath his unassuming exterior. They come to the fore wherever and whenever they are required. Any female in need of such will be more than satisfied.

The Hermit-nature is trustworthy, like the proverbial

Dutch uncle. The rampart, domineering Charioteer may not kiss and tell, but the fact of sexual conquest will show in his demeanor and often on his face, like the cat that ate the canary. But the Hermit-nature will never reveal anything. His countenance and bearing will conceal the fact of sexual escapades forever. This secretive quality greatly enhances the Hermit-nature's desirability. Secretiveness, coupled with his unassuming behavior, makes the Hermit-nature an ideal bed partner for love-hungry housewives. The Hermit-nature is not unattainable, the true mystical meaning of the eminence and the beacon. The card says: What I know and experience, you also may know and experience.

In a reading this card means: Sexual enjoyment of the highest degree; attainment of libidinal knowledge; understanding of the needs and desires of the opposite sex; prudence in illicit affairs.

WHEEL of FORTUNE.

X

Wheel of Fortune

Inscribed on the wheel is the transliteration of TARO *as* ROTA. *The counterchanging letters signify the divine name. . . .*

SEXUAL KEY Basically, the Wheel means that life as we know it is a constant fluctuation and is in a constant state of change, i.e., tumescence and flaccidity; passion and passivity; celibacy and hypersexuality; love and hate. The Divine Name signifies that unchangeable Providence exists throughout life's changes.

. . . A serpentine creature flanks the left of the Wheel while the Wheel itself seems to be supported by a fiery-red lupine creature. A blue sphinx, holding a sword, sits atop the Wheel. . . .

SEXUAL KEY The elongated form of the snake symbolizes the constancy of penile utility and genital activity as an apropos form of man's expression. The lupine creature represents the raw animal passions of man as a separate entity from penile administrations and sexual intercourse (the snake), implying that passion need not necessarily be satiated or appeased. On the other hand, it signifies that both lust and sexual activity are counterparts and that each follows the other endlessly. The sphinx is emblematic of stability amidst fluctuation and symbolizes the immutability of the phallus amidst changing mores and ethics. This certainty is signified by the blue color of the sphinx, blue once again denoting mastery, leadership, attainment. The sword is power.

. . . The four corners are occupied by winged characters, each of which is reading a book. . . .

SEXUAL KEY Sexual knowledge is not always obtained experientally. More often than not such knowledge is acquired through the reading of books on the subject. As long as man has eyes there will be books. The wings of the creatures denote flight to knowledge, the salvation of mankind. The two characters of the lower corners are animals, depicting man's baser, beastly nature, and the books they read, the knowledge of sex they acquire, are often detrimental to them. Above, occupying the two higher corners of the card, are a bird and what appears to be an angel but is not. It is man in yet another form, at another stage. All four symbols mean man, in different stages. The two above are higher and achieve stature by reading books on the subject of sex which reach the inner man and teach of unselfish sex. The message of the lower characters is: sex for me. The message of the higher characters is: sex for us.

SEXUAL SIGNIFICATION
OF THE WHEEL OF FORTUNE CARD

Life's ups and downs are symbolized herein. The card says that though a person has his cake and is eating it too (which *is* possible), such a state of ecstasy cannot be prolonged indefinitely. Though sexuality is here to stay, each person cannot enjoy it always. Though male and female genitalia shall always meet, individual men and women (as in an illicit affair), cannot expect their genitalia always to meet. What is universally true is not individually changeless. The passion-symbolizing creature followed by the phallus-symbolizing snake suggests that the confluence of passion and phallus is what makes the world go round. In a never-ending cycle of desire, gratification, desire, gratification, man pursues woman and woman pursues man.

In a reading this card means: Ever-changing sexual partners, changeable sexual proclivities; new and interesting cohabiters; success in sexual pursuits; an increase of sexual partners. The turning, hence changing, aspect of the Wheel, advises: Face changes in partners with courage; be alert for sexual opportunities; exercise caution in coital excesses; maintain sexual equilibrium; guard against discordant members of the opposite sex. Further renderings are: Patience in passion will be rewarded; new sexual contacts require adaptability; unexpected escapades may occur.

XI

Justice

A crowned woman is seated upon a throne
between two pillars, an upright sword in
her right hand, a pair of scales suspended
from her left hand. Behind her, a purple curtain.

SEXUAL KEY   That she is crowned denotes excellence, attainment, leadership. The darkened pillars, phallic symbols, are depicted without burgeoning heads and orgasmic proportions. The upright sword in her right hand, though symbolizing the male sexual organ, is also darkened. The scales express the need for equality and balance.

SEXUAL SIGNIFICATION
OF THE JUSTICE CARD

The word Justice itself speaks out for balance and equilibrium in sexual affairs. Therefore, the message of the darkened phalli is that they arrived at this state through sexual intemperance. Their orgasmic heads are not honored here for these represent unruly and indiscriminate male sexual organs which have and will penetrate any orifice without regard for the higher law of moderation. The Justice-nature disapproves of lawless genitals but she does not deny the supremacy of the phallus, particularly in its erected form, which infers sexual foreplay on her part and therefore a tempering of even her hypercritical spirit. The Justice-nature cannot be coerced into sexual intercourse but will give freely of her body and passion to the deserving. She will not respond to a stolen or forced kiss, but will melt in the arms of an ardent suitor, who, in the face of all odds, has adamantly pursued her favor.

The Justice-nature believes labor should be rewarded and she will see to it that a man gets what he has diligently worked for. On the other hand, the Justice-nature does not believe that a man should enjoy sex simply because sex exists. When this nature has two suitors, because of her sense of equality and justice, both will taste the fruits of their labor. When her sense of probity blankets ten men, however, this nature experiences hardships, is often accused of sexual immoderation and promiscuity, which in a higher sense is not true. She merely gives each man his just deserts.

The Justice-nature will not give of her body, passion, love, or sexuality until she feels it is right and just. She is very critical of animal passion and derives no pleasure from aggressive phalli no matter how gross or esthetic, but the phallus which justly deserves her submission will find her more passionate than the lustiest of females.

In a spread this card means: Equity of passion; rightness of dispersed affection; probity in selection of sexual mates. It suggests that sexual activity is directly proportionate to sexual pursuit, that orgasmic ecstasy is not a plaything but an equitable result for armorous labor.

THE HANGED MAN.

XII

The Hanged Man

There is a nimbus about the head of the seeming martyr, who is suspended from a cruciform gallows.

SEXUAL KEY   The tree itself is a phallic symbol, but rather than terminating in a *glans penis,* it ends with a crossbar, denoting cessation of sexual activity. That the crossbar bears living foliage suggests that though the phallus is inactive, it is not dead. The hanged man, it should be noted, suggests life in suspension, but life and not death, as is often erroneously concluded. This is suspended sexuality, not asexuality or impotence.

SEXUAL SIGNIFICATION
OF THE HANGED MAN CARD

The Hanged Man is a card of profound significance, but all the significance is veiled, often by misinterpretation of one's initial view of the card, and by the card's name. It should be noted that the hanged man's face does not express suffering, but entrancement. This is the card of all sexual narcissists into which category all masturbators fall. The Hanged Man-nature, early in life, adopts an idea of what his penis should look like, feel like, function like, respond like, and act like, notwithstanding biological facts to the contrary. This is the card of self-lovers who feel their genitals are meant for some great and grand purpose, usually other than sexual intercourse. Thus the nimbus about the Hanged Man's head. This nature would rather have the head of his organ (*glans penis,* clitoris) "martyred" than functioning in an unworthy manner. This nature usually experiences a post-pubertal collision with the "facts of life" and is henceforth disillusioned. Since these "facts of life" do not conform with this nature's idealistic outlook, it would rather suffer celibacy.

Some of this nature turn to chronic masturbation, finding autoerotism more to their liking than heterosexual activities with the impassioned and demanding sexual organs of the opposite sex. Some do nothing at all, suspending their sexuality temporarily and perhaps enjoying only nocturnal emissions. The Hanged Man-nature thinks "all women (men) are alike." He feels that the opposite sex does not understand him, which is true because they are normal, red-blooded humans who desire their fires of passion extinguished regularly. Further, the Hanged Man-nature arrives at his suspension of sexuality in a unique manner. He sees Woman (Man) as ideal and places the opposite sex on a pedestal, but, during maturation, he stumbles over the sex act, finding it impossible to reconcile orgiastic passion and pulsating organs with serene perfection and Utopian bliss.

In a reading this card suggests a dreamer who cannot accept everyday sexual responsibility, and though this card denotes a person of indecision, it also represents an individual at the crossroads of ideal and actual sex.

It represents youth (chronological or psychological) in need of sexual guidance and sex education. The Hanged Man-nature is one worthy of a female's (male's) patience and understanding, for with the proper guidance this nature can become a veritable dynamo in the sexual bed. The card in a spread also means: Too much discernment in sexual matters; trials with the opposite sex; sacrifice of sexual pleasure for ideals; emotional sorrow; sexual disappointment. This card advises the Hanged Man-nature forgive the opposite sex their "infirmities"; choose a sexual partner only after taking into consideration your tendency to expect too much; apply the imagination and not idealism to a prospective assignation. This card further intimates an awakening after suspension and predicts the possibility of a highly pleasurable sexual future.

XIII

Death

*A mysterious horseman moves slowly, carrying
a black flag on which is represented the
mystic rose. He carries no visible weapon
and yet one man is fallen, a prelate awaits
his end with clasped hands, and a child and
a maiden kneel before him. In the background
is a flowing river and two pillars between
which the sun shines radiantly.*

SEXUAL KEY   As with the card of the Hanged Man, the
card of Death must be explained. It does not mean
death in the common sense of the word, for no mere
card can predict the physical cessation of life. The
Death card signifies change, transformation, and passage
from lower to higher. The Mystic Rose emblazoned on
the banner signifies ever-blossoming vaginas, and the
sun, between two phallic symbols, represents ever-rising
phalli, so, mystically, the Death card does not predict
doom. It does, however, predict an end to something.
The fallen king, for example, has lived to see the end
of his rulership, his crown removed. This could very

well be the Charioteer-nature, after his heyday. The snail-like form in front of the child and the maiden symbolizes the slowness (as some men count time) but the certainty that a penis will reach them both. Eventuality is the message of the snail-phallic. It is highly symbolic of death and of life, denoting the death of the little girl's childhood and the birth of her puberty. Behind the child, the young maiden modestly turns her head from Death and the phallic symbol, as though turning her head from the fact of life that her hymen is to be ruptured, her vagina to be penetrated by the heretofore dreamed-of penis. She shall witness the death of her maidenhood and the birth of womanhood. The prelate, unkneeling, of the Hierophant-nature, is not quick to accept change and therefore attempts to pray his way out of the inevitable. The flowing river, again symbolizing the incessant effluence of vaginal and penile excretions, denotes life, change, and progress.

SEXUAL SIGNIFICATION
OF THE DEATH CARD

A Death-nature is a "changer." The change may be welcomed or unwelcomed. Illustrative of the former is a desired lover; of the latter, unexpected or ill-received sexual attention, as from a rapist. Death signifies the gamut of sexual perversions in that the card denotes the inevitability of change, whether desired or not. Therefore, the Death-nature may very well be a sexually perverted person. Change or transformation, however, does not always occur in a perverted manner. It may also occur as a matter of growth. The presence of the Death card may foretell imminent change in one's life. Therefore, a young virgin who knows full well that she shall not be virginal forever, can, by the upturning of the Death card, prepare herself for the object of her desires, or, should she prefer, she can be forewarned by the Death card and postpone the loss of her virginity. Likewise, the pubescent boy, desiring to be a "man," may, by the upturning of the card, realize the proximity of impending sexual intercourse. The Death card is as often good as bad, for whereas it may foretell the cessation of some supposed sexual happiness in one reading, it may foretell the cessation of sexual despair in another. The despairing female, a slave to the passions of a bestial mate, may be blessed by the presence of the Death card which promises an end to her sexual slavery; and the frustrated female, despairing for lack of sexual intercourse, may realize renewed hope of deliverance from the bonds of chastity by the presence of the Death card.

In a spread this card means: End, finish (which, as explained, foretells birth, beginning); great change in sexual atmosphere; transformation of sexual expression, from lower to higher; the conclusion of part of one's sex life will make way for new vistas of sensual pleasure; a new sexual venture; death of sexual selfishness; death of autoerotism and birth of sexual activity; new and vigorous sexual organs imminent. The card further denotes: Faced with a door to new ecstasy; energetic sexual activity; end of a despairing sex life; new creative trends of libido. The free will of man is demonstrated in a further rendering of the Death card. A person who faithfully and diligently seeks change may find this card in a spread as "an answer to prayer." In such a case the card's message is: Change your thoughts and you change your life.

XIV

Temperance

A winged angel with the solar sign upon its
head and a framed triangle upon its breast,
is pouring fluid from chalice to chalice.
A rainbow arcs over its wings. . . .

SEXUAL KEY   The angel symbolizes a higher knowledge of human nature and its sexual behavior, neither condoning it nor condemning it, representing the mystical Neutrality. The solar sign signifies life; that is, birth and rebirth, procreation and reproduction. The arcing rainbow is emblematic of the divine promise that man shall never again perish by water; that is, the seminal fluids of copulating Mankind will not again be cause of an inundation of sinfulness. The triangle within a square symbolizes Consummate Vagina. The fluid which the angel pours symbolizes effusive female excretion and ejaculatory male semen, the very essences of life. One would be hard put to tell in whch direction the fluid is running and where the female and male meet. Tribades erroneously interpret the fluid as female liquescence only, manifested during their genital-to-genital perversion. The fluid is male and female orgasmic juices, ever-intermingling, ever interflowing.

... The angel has one foot in the water
and one foot upon the earth. ...

SEXUAL KEY This is highly illustrative of the very meaning of Temperance; that is, tempering earth (fleshly desire) with water (seminal fluids). It is the mixture which produces orgasmic fruit, for it is the one which causes the other. It is the watering of the earth which produces flowers of sexual joy.

... Beyond the angel a path arises to certain
heights on the verge of the horizon. Above,
a crown is vaguely seen through a great light.

SEXUAL KEY The path symbolizes the ascendant greatness and nobility of orgasms from sexual experience to sexual experience. The great light and the crown denote the culmination of all sexual experience in superior sexual knowledge, like unto the Neutral angel's, that is, neither condoning nor condemning human nature or its sexual behavior.

SEXUAL SIGNIFICATION
OF THE TEMPERANCE CARD

The Temperance-nature never bites off more than it can chew; its orgasmic delights are directly proportionate to impassioned desire, overindulging in neither. Harmony of biological need and emotional desire is enjoyed by this nature through the practices of sexual self-control and the discipline of fleshly appetites. The reward for such a regimen is symbolized by the ascendant path, for the Temperance-nature, though temperate in individual sexual excursions, enjoys successively finer and more satisfying orgasms. This nature knows that the heights of sexual and sensual pleasure are not reached successfully and gratifyingly by helter-skelter, impetuous, intemperate flight into wild and vicious sex acts, but rather by gourmet-like tastes, snail-like deliberation, and astute dissemination of coitus.

In a spread this card means: Life will be balanced, with all sexual pursuits bearing the fruit of satiating orgasms; balanced sexual expression; wild orgasms and tame orgasms enjoyed with equanimitiy. It also foretells sexual goals reached through wisdom; orgasms achieved through circumspect courtship; sexual balance is ultimately rewarded with ecstasy. It warns: Temper burning lusts with therapeutic copulation; coite no oftener than passion dictates.

THE DEVIL .

XV

The Devil

*Standing on a black altar is a horned goat
with the wings of a bat. The right hand is
open and in the left hand there is a great
flaming torch, inverted. A reversed pentagram
is on the beast's forehead. There are
two figures, one male, one female, chained
to the altar. The figures are tailed, the
female with fruit, the male with fire.*

SEXUAL KEY The black altar symbolizes the meta-
phorical altar of supreme sacrifice where male and
female relinquish their right to wholesome and healthy
sexuality. The horned goat, or Devil, represents the
baser side of human nature. He symbolizes raw sexual
craving, lust, inordinate desires, sexual perversion, evil
thoughts, desires, and deeds. The open right hand de-
ceivingly suggests that sex is its own justification and
needs no other, that there is naught but sex as a basis
for living. It implies that there is no higher calling, no
elevated human nature, no freedom from the bonds of
lust and sexual depravity. The wings on the Devil mean

night and darkness, for the bat is a nocturnal creature. The wings symbolize that time and place when depravity and wickedness are best manifested; that is, at night, in darkness, surreptitiously, clandestinely, secretly. The flaming torch in the left hand denotes the animal nature of humankind, the burning lust and fiery passions of the depraved. The torch is inverted so as to light the consuming fires of sexual deviation, sadism, bestiality, and inhuman degeneracy.

The inverted pentagram is the symbol for excellence, but excellence in perverse sexuality. This bastard crown is for those who neither aspire for nor believe in the crown of gold. The two figures are chained to the altar of infamy, but take note how loosely the chains are hung about their necks. These chains can be readily removed but only by themselves, by an act of will. As long as they keep their chains they shall grow the horns of animalism. The man's tail of fire symbolizes the flames of vice and corruption which catapult him into sexual excess and debauchery. It is by this fire that the depraved woman bears fruit, symbolized by her tail; red fruit of blood and passion which drive her on and on to greater and greater sexual evils.

SEXUAL SIGNIFICATION
OF THE DEVIL CARD

The Devil-nature, as opposed to the nature of the preceding card, always bites off more than he or she can chew. This nature seeks orgasms compulsively, as though driven by some inner demon which cannot be sated. The Devil-nature mistakes quantity for quality and it therefore copulates indiscriminately. A man of this nature will stop at nothing to achieve orgasm. He holds nothing sacred, and to gain his end he will defile a virgin, rape the wife of a friend by guile or force, debase a young girl or force her to practice fellatio upon him. If all else fails he will turn to sodomy or pederasty, even bestiality. Orgasm is his god.

Under circumstances prohibiting sexual partners, the Devil-nature will indulge in every autoerotic practice known to man, from masturbation to the introduction of foreign objects into his anal cavity. Any and all erogenous zones are put into full play in the name of orgasm. Likewise in the female of this nature. She, seemingly insatiable, will seduce even the youngest of boys when necessary. No man is safe from this nature's greedy sexuality. She will vamp any married man, any single man. If she is married, her marriage is used as a front for extramarital relations with friends and strangers alike. Her own husband's brothers and father are fair game in her quest for orgasm. As with her male counterpart, the Devil-nature will, when all else fails, achieve her indispensable orgasms via whatever means available to her, barring nothing. She is not above turning to a pet for sexual gratification, be it canine or feline. Failing this, no phallic-shaped object is beyond her use vaginally and anally. The Devil card is the card of nymphomaniacs, satyrs, the incestuous, the hypersexuals. Secondly, it is the card of those who, notwithstanding an apparently acceptable way of life, compulsively harbor evil thoughts and daily indulge in fantasies of a perverse nature. Thirdly, it is the card of Man, in his stage of animalism, the stage which can be passed or surmounted only by an act of will.

In a reading this card means: Triumph by deceit; amatory successes and orgasmic riches obtained by trickery and dishonest means; destruction of others. The Devil-card implies, however, that sexual triumph will be temporary and that it will be followed by a talion punishment. In short, evil sexuality brings on damaging results, not only to the sexually abused, but to the sexual perpetrator. The card also means: perverse sexual life; disregard for human dignity; erotic vehemence; ravage; violence; weakness of will; blindness to the needs of others; pettiness. This is the card of the Marquis de Sade, of Lucretia Borgia, of sex criminals. In a less vibrant sense, it is the card of all, for as humans we possess a dark side.

THE TOWER.

XVI

The Tower

A bolt of lightning has struck a grey tower,
dislodging its crown and setting it in flames.
Two figures fall from the flaming building.

SEXUAL KEY   The card has dual meaning throughout.
The bolt of lightning, because it comes from above, is
firstly Authority, and secondly, Intellect. The tower is
first a penis and secondly a House of Sexual Doctrine.
The crown is the physical pre-eminence of that Doctrine, and also symbolic of the glans penis. The two
figures, on the one hand, are living sufferers of the
destruction, and, on the other hand, they symbolize the
male and female aspects of one individual. That the
Tower card depicts ruin is obvious. It is the rending
of the House of Sexual Doctrine; that is, the ruination
of concepts and practices which have been harmful.
Alternately, it depicts the destruction of the false penis;
that is, the bestial, unloving, orgasm-motivated phallus.
The grey color, too, speaks of waning virility and utility.
The message is: Unless Love erect the penis (clitoris),
they labor in vain who erect it. The Tower card speaks

of the chastisement of the sexually proud and the instinctually perverted. In a sense, the catastrophe is a reflection from the Devil card, the talion punishment for selfish, base, and lascivious living. It is not necessarily a bad card, despite its ominous apeparance. It depends upon the Querent in whose reading it occurs. It may predict the intrusion of law-enforcement authorities into a life of perverse libertinism, or it may predict the light of reason and intellect into an otherwise depraved existence. The former can be a curse, the latter a blessing. The falling figures, in a positive reading, could mean the falling from sexual depravity; the fall to be followed by sexual bliss. In a negative reading, as in the case of an obdurate vice king, the figures can mean a falling to destruction; that is, prison, or even death.

SEXUAL SIGNIFICATION
OF THE TOWER CARD

The Tower-nature has been riding high sexually at the expense of others. Because this nature's sexual habits and propensities are damaging to others, a price must be paid for its enforced and stolen joys. A harvest of ill-gotten orgasms, no matter how enjoyable at the time, requires the rapacious recipient to pay.

In a reading this card means: Cessation of sexual activities; loss of sexual prowess and power; sexual abuse abruptly halted; castration; venereal disease; shattered dreams of sexual fame; self-imposed celibacy; disgrace; ruin; adversity; distress; misery. It can also mean: Freedom from the bonds of lust; re-evaluation of one's mores; and the end of sexual slavery; sudden and rejuvenating love.

THE STAR.

XVII

The Star

Seven white stars surround a golden radiant star. A naked female is in the foreground, her right foot upon water, her left knee upon earth. She irrigates land and sea by pouring liquid from two pitchers. Behind her is a red bird alighting on a tree.

SEXUAL KEY The seven white stars, of lesser magnitude than the eighth, signify the seven aspects of man's sexuality: infantilism, narcissism, fetishism, perversion, desire, passion, love. The eighth star symbolizes the radiant stage of man's sexuality, and it incorporates all seven of the lesser aspects in perfect unity and balance and it signifies sexual maturity. The naked female characterizes Woman, open to Man, without whom life would cease. Her body, symbolized by her knee and foot, marks the interrelation of earth (fleshly desire) and water (seminal fluid). The two pitchers represent phalli, male and female, and the Star freely pours orgasmic juices, irrigating desire and orgasm that both may flourish. The motto of the card is: Fluids of life freely given. The tree behind her signifies life and growth. The bird represents the human phallus, penis and clitoris, like the nightingale of Boccacio's *Decameron*. Its red color is obvious in its allusion.

SEXUAL SIGNIFICATION
OF THE STAR CARD

The Star-nature "has been everywhere and done everything," and has learned well from its experiences. This nature is the true lover. If a partner has a fetish, he or she is not castigated for it. The mere fact of fetishism is cultivated and the sexual relationship is thereby greatly enhanced. The Star-nature makes its mate feel truly wanted, needed, and loved. This nature promises sexual bliss. No sex act is denied. Fetishism, perversion, narcissism—these and more are utilized expertly and in tactful doses, enriching the sex acts and ultimately the relationship. The Star-nature is one of hope and good luck, a light in anyone's life, truly a star in the long night of bed-hopping.

In a spread this card means: Love of sex; physical love; sexual harmony; erotic inspiration; new perception of physical and sexual things; good health; virility; strength and potency; new lease on life; hope and bright sexual prospects.

© Lorillard 1973

Micronite filter.
Mild, smooth taste.
America's quality
cigarette.
Kent.

King Size or Deluxe 100's.

Try the crisp, clean taste of Kent Menthol.

The only Menthol with the famous Micronite filter.

THE MOON.

XVIII

The Moon

The moon is shown above and beyond two pillars. Between the pillars is a path. In the foreground are three creatures: a dog, a wolf, and a creeping thing which comes out of the water.

SEXUAL KEY   The moon represents reflected light; that is, dimmed sexual knowledge. It drops dew of flames as if to burn those beneath it. The two pillars form a gate of entry, implying that phallicism is the way to life. The dog and the wolf symbolize lust and dark passion respectively. The crayfish represents the hideous sexual tendencies of those whose propensities are lower than those of the savage beast. The water, at once orgasmic fluids, also suggests the depths of depravity some men plumb in their voracious quest for orgasm.

SEXUAL SIGNIFICATION
OF THE MOON CARD

Those of the Moon-nature lack conscience and therefore indulge rather naively in sexual perversion. This nature has little understanding of the value of love. They have a sense of fear of true love and, like lambs to the slaughter, are easily led into damnable sexual relationships. The Moon-natures manifest a false joy for the sake of onlookers. These are the "swingers," the "lives of the party," those who exhibit for public view a life of pesudo-sexual freedom. In privacy, away from a public, lights, and exhibitionism, this nature experiences great fear and dread. Aloneness is their enemy, for it is in the dark of night that they see ghosts and spirits, all specters of themselves. They keep horrific secrets and make a pretense of serenity and inner peace. They actually fear the shadows of their own minds, for it is hidden in those shadows that they see themselves as lurking beasts.

The Moon-nature does not necessarily lie, but it always conceals. The Moon-nature is terribly insecure, is often neurotic, and sometimes psychotic. Most paraphiliacs are Moon-natures, endeavoring to escape and conceal truth by recklessly engaging in such sexual perversions as pedophilia, sadomasochism, oralism, sodomy, and gerontophilia. Pryromaniacs are among the Moon-natures. Each perversion to the Moon-nature is escape; sexual activity for the sake of diversion. They invariably mistake action for progress and growth and they abhor inactivity as though it were death itself. Lacking insight and higher ideals, this nature is easily lured into vileness and is easy prey for seasonal sexual perverts.

In a reading this card means: Unforeseen perils to sexuality; danger to sexual security; insanity may follow great mental instability; playful perversion may lead to perilous paraphilia; illusory love; a scandal or secret betrayed; inactive conscience; slander; sickness; hidden enemies; calumny; deceptive sexual partners; error in mating: darkness; terror. There can be a bright side to this card in that the moon is increasing to the right of the observer on what is called the side of mercy. In this case, the card represents life of reality apart from life of fantasy, and the path between the phallic symbols is the entrance into the unknown.

The animals symbolize the fears of the fantastic natural mind in the presence of that gate, particularly when there is only reflected light to guide it. The moon is reflecting the guiding light of conscience and beyond it is the unknown which it cannot illuminate because that which lies beyond is a mystery, a potential finale for those who relentlessly pursue a life of sexual perversion. The card has two forces at work. The moon illuminates the animal nature which is responsible for unnatural lusts, and the creeping thing, man's hideous sexual tendencies, strives to attain power, symbolized by crawling from the liquid abyss. If it were to succeed, the Moon-nature could commit horrible murders or perpetrate the lowest of perversions—necrophilia, but, as a rule, the crayfish sinks back. The face of reflected conscience directs a calm gaze upon the sexual tumult below and it may be that the wild animal nature will be calmed, while the creeping horror shall cease striving to manifest itself. The Moon card then may mean: Peace; sexual visions become sexual reality; calmness of libido; victory of conscience and self-control over animal passion and sexual perversity. The Moon card in a spread often serves as a warning. Fear, symbolized by the crayfish, and borne of man's depravity, can be

driven back to the place from which it had no right to
emerge, the imagination. Love, after the capacity to
love is almost destroyed by lust and fear of evil desires,
may win out.

THE SUN .

XIX

The Sun

Mounted on a white horse is a naked child.
He displays a red banner. Behind him is a
black wall and bossoming flowers. A bright
sun shines upon all.

SEXUAL KEY   The sun radiates strength and symbolizes renewal of consciousness above the natural mind. The lad represents the heart of a child; that is, base humanity has become like a child—innocent in the sense of wise, a child in the sense of simplicity. The horse represents man's potential sexual power. The wall symbolizes dark thoughts, deeds, and desires which confront man and bar him from the higher realization of the meaning of sex. Flowers of fruitful orgasms, and leaves of love, blossom nevertheless. The red banner of passion and sexual need is flown innocently by the child as only a child in its simplicity can do. The naked child, unashamed of his needs or of his sexual organs, has mounted the horse which symbolizes his reign over animal nature. Any man, activating his conscience, becomes as a little child, and thereby reigns over his unchecked passions. He becomes renewed. He may then lead forth his animal nature, his Devil-nature, not in captivity, which is repression, but in a state of perfect conformity.

SEXUAL SIGNIFICATION
OF THE SUN CARD

The Sun-nature has received the direct light of conscience. This nature's darkest thoughts create no debilitating fear for it knows from experience that love conquers all. The Sun-nature enters into wholesome sexual relations and is a great lover. It activates and de-activates its animal nature at will and does not allow them to cloud its reason. The Sun-nature produces abundant orgasms but for lover's sake. Sexual activity conforms to love's dictates. Love, not lust, excites the genitals. Mutual orgasm and reciprocal ecstasy are musts for this nature.

In a spread this card means: Sexual happiness; Cyprian contentment; fortunate unions; triumph and success in sexual endeavors; assured orgasms; completion of all copulations; pleasure in simple sex; healthy coition. This card further signifies the transit from the love of this world, represented by sexual orientation, to the love of the world to come, typified by the innocent heart of a child.

JUDGEMENT.

XX

Judgment

*An angel sounds his bannered trumpet and
men, women, and children arise
from black caskets.*

SEXUAL KEY   The angel symbolizes conscience and the
trumpet produces the voice of conscience. All men respond, naked and unashamed. Their bodies are grey in
color denotes the subjugation of carnal desire. The
people appear to be adoring, ecstatic. At the call of
conscience, some men and women, children at heart,
arise from coffins of perversion and prisons of sexual
slavery. Judgment is the card symbolizing the accom-
plishment of the great work of transformation in reply
to the summons of conscience, the summons which is
heard and answered from within. The card implies actual judgment only in the sense that every man must
eventually judge himself. Indeed, when the summons is
sounded, man must judge himself, must make a choice
by effort of will. The pedophiliac is called from his
sexual abuse of little girls; the pederast is invited away
from anal intercourse with young boys; the depraved

woman is requested to cease her immoral sexual practices; the lecher is called from his extortion of sexual intercourse. Whether they respond or not is up to them. Not all caskets open.

SEXUAL SIGNIFICATION
OF THE JUDGMENT CARD

The Judgment-nature is on the threshold of discovery and choice. No matter what his present sexual habit may be, if it is wrong for him or harmful to others, he will hear a call from within. Heeded, it promises a safer, saner sex life. Unheeded, it spells disaster. Those with a hardness of heart tantamount to the hardness of their penis (clitoris) are headed for disaster. Those who yield to the call soon have something to which they can relate their old life. They receive new sexual perspective, renewed virility, fresh sex partners, and the past life takes on the appearance of death itself. Heeding the summons, these individuals rise from tombs of errant sex practices.

In a spread this card means: Regeneration of virility and the sexual organs after a period of suffering and waste; sexual friendships multiplied; gratifying orgasms through sex well done; sexual judgment in one's favor; change of sexual tastes; renewed interet in wholesome sexualitiy; passion rekindled; freedom from sexual imprisonment; new, prolonged orgasms.

THE WORLD.

XXI

The World

*Centrally located is a naked woman whose
vagina is concealed. She holds a pair of
wands, each double-headed. Around her is
a green wreathlike oval bearing red entwinings.
The corners each have a figure.*

SEXUAL KEY The physical world in all its glory. The
four figures symbolize the four elements and are
analagous to the Tarot symbols: Wand-Fire (Lust,
Anger, Passion); Cup-Water (Urine, Blood, Semen);
Sword-Earth (Flesh, Force, Malleability); and,
Pentacle-Air (Flatus, Eructation, Respiration). The
green of the woman's enclosure represents fecundity.
The red indicates periodical menstruation. That the
woman's genitals are concealed by a purple banner
means that Woman, in the universal sense, has her
vagina sated by phalli purple with use. This woman,
then, is all women, or the Ideal Woman. Herein she
is depicted holding two phallic symbols gingerly, almost
playfully. They are the toys of Woman. The symbolism
behind the four heads of the phalli is Woman's insatiety.

73

She can receive four phalli—one to be masturbated by hand, one to be fellated, another for vaginal penetration, the fourth for anal intercourse. She can take them one at a time or all four simultaneously. She can bring all four to frenetic orgasm. The card denotes Woman's capacity to accept four phalli at once, and then four more, and four more, *ad infinitum*. She appears to be dancing, a carefree young woman, and therein she is the personification of Fun, Pleasure, Excitement, Gaiety, Hypersexuality. The sexual elements around her, symbolized by the four figures, are implemented for her diversions.

SEXUAL SIGNIFICATION
OF THE WORLD CARD

The World-nature rides high on the waves of Paphian joy. This nature has "the world by the tail," "life in the palm of her hand." For a woman of this nature, the card typifies her personality and not her thoughts. She identifies with the sexual rendering. For a man of this nature, the card represents his thoughts and not his personality—an infinity of erotic pleasures.

In a spread this card means: Femininity; complete pleasure; erotic fulfillment; Fescennine success; triumphant sensuality; sexual desires sated; amatory excellence; assured coitus; change of sexual partners; flights from the unerotic; voyage upon the sea of sensuous delight. In a man's reading, this card represents the way he thinks of women. In a female's reading it represents herself.

THE FOOL.

0

The Fool

Light of step, as though obstacles in life
do not exist, a gaily dressed young man
pauses at the brink of a precipice. He is
in motion, though stationary at the moment.
His dog is still romping. The youth looks
skyward, unterrorized by the depths which
open before him, as though falling from
the precipice was impossible. He has a long
wand in one hand, from which hangs over his
right shoulder a sack. In his left hand is
a white rose. The sun shining
behind him is white.

SEXUAL KEY   He is the spirit of youth in search of
sexual experience. He represents the sensate life, the
world of the flesh. He symbolizes the phallic stage of
human development wherein everything in life is seen
as sexually based, wherein sexual activity is the only

endeavor worthy of effort, wherein sex is the solution for every problem. The rose he carries emblemizes the vagina, white for purity, blossomed for penetration. The wand typifies the Fool's version of the penis, its length symbolic of size and duration. The sack hanging from the phallic symbol represents the scrotum, which the Fool sees as a veritable "semen factory." The world below him is the world of responsible action and higher ideals. The white sun, maturity in symbolism, knows, him, knows where he came from, where he is going, and how he will return via the path of sexual knowledge after many days.

SEXUAL SIGNIFICATION
OF THE FOOL CARD

The Fool-nature is in love with sex. No matter his chronological age, the Fool-nature is an impetuous youth with an enlongated penis, a scrotum filled with semen, an itch for coitus, and a Pollyanna concept of sexuality. He cherishes the indefatigable capactiy of his scrotum and testicles to produce abundant semen and he adores his penis. He deifies the sex act. The Fool-nature, in short, is Freudian in every sense of the world. He develops a *penis erectus* at every opportunity, and he feels every hole should be filled. The Fool-nature is the counterpart of the World-nature. For a man of this nature the card represents his personality. For a woman, it represents her thoughts concerning men.

In a reading this card means: Journey through sexual life; sexual independence; erotic adventures; blind concupiscence; sexual forces in full play; psychosexual creativity; will to orgasm; rebellion against sexual taboos; undisciplined erotism; thoughtless sexual escapades; phallic-worship; hypersexuality; orgasmic extravagance; licentious folly; erotomania; intoxicating ecstasy; sexual and sensual delirium; satyriasis. In a male's reading it represents himself. In a female's reading it represents her view of men at large.

Part Two

THE LESSER ARCANA
AND THEIR AUGURIES

The Lesser Arcana consists of 56 cards corresponding to the modern playing cards, plus four Knights. These cards are complementary to the Major Arcana. Indeed, as will be seen in a spread, the more Major Trumps present the more meaning have the Lesser Arcana. These 56 cards, if you will, are extensions of the 22 Major Trumps. They ameliorate or intensify a Major Trump card and its meaning. They add to or detract from the message of the cards.

KING ♦ CUPS.

The Suit of Cups

KING

Auguries: A man, fair of complexion, endowed with an esthetic phallus; he is a man of responsibility and does not shirk his sexual duties; a man disposed to oblige the Querent's sexual needs, his love objects are usually church-going females; also, a businessman or a man skilled in law; also, creative sexuality.

Inverted: A double-dealing man; a liar; a seducer; also, a businessman who uses his power and authority to extort sex; a cuckold; also, false love to gain orgasm; dishonesty in sexual relations; erotic exaction; two-facedness; scandal; vice; loss of virginity or reputation; impotence.

QUEEN

Auguries: A woman, fair in form and figure; a dreamer who also acts; a woman of rich sexual powers; a romantic woman; a woman who will sexually serve the Querent; a perfect mistress or lover; a woman who encourages coitus and gains pleasure from the orgasms of others; she has wild sexual fantasies but she is practical in bed; also, sensual happiness, success, pleasure.

QUEEN of CUPS.   KNIGHT of CUPS.

Inverted: Perverse woman; a woman skilled in the art of sexual pleasure but one not to be trusted; a beautiful and sensuous woman who can lead a man to financial ruin; a "homebreaker"; also sexual perversion; vice; depraved activities for self-gain; a fellatress; a scrotolinctress; analinguist; a woman who engages in paraphilia for personal aggrandizement.

KNIGHT

Auguries: A young man, sexually imaginative; also, the beginning of new sexual relationships; provocative proposals; sexual arrival; excitement; amatory advances; new throes of passion; sex in the name of business; lascivious propositions; invitations to the sexual bed; new contacts; message of impending joy; hopeful orgasms; a fresh new phallus.

PAGE of CUPS.

Inverted: A wife-seducer; a pedophiliac; trickery; a sex-swindler; a fraud; a sly and cunning young man whose only aim is to rape and deflower; duplicity; artificial friendship for sexual gain.

PAGE

Auguries: An effeminate young man; a catamite; a youth impelled to render sexual service and with whom the Querent will be sexually united; a young lover; also, news of invigorating copulation; reflection, meditation, and application directed to sexuality; new conquests.

Inverted: A deceptive young man; a rebellious youth; a gay seducer; the lover of young girls whom all mothers dread; a young defiler of mothers and wives who takes advantage of alcoholically or drug-induced intoxication; false friendship for sexual gain.

TEN

Auguries: Carnal contentment; sexual perfection; perfect sexual unions; fruitful orgasms; perfect states of erection, clitoral and penile; genital harmony; suc-

cessful sexual pursuits; repose of the libido; if with several Trumps Major, a person who will take charge of the Querent's sexual interests; also, the atmosphere, miasma, or circumstances of the sexually inclined Querent.

Inverted: Hysterical passion; corrupt love; criminal sexuality; rape, sexual extortion; forced orgasm; drastic sexual involvement; licentious rage; fanatical phallic-worship; abused genitals; sexual violence.

NINE

Auguries: Sexual goodwill; satisfaction and happiness with one's erotism; also, victory of passion over reluctant sex partners; copulative success; abundant orgasm; physical and erogenous wealth; advantage over sexual competitors; also, sexual delight for the Querent.

Inverted: Mistakes in sexual technique; coital imperfections; false pride, too great a sense of sexual prowess; danger of impotence; possible lack of sexual mates; sentimentality over a sexual relationship leading to isolation and masturbation.

EIGHT

Auguries: Sexual timidity; shyness; unnatural fear of plentiful orgasms; amatory meekness; modesty causing sexual isolation; enjoyment of masturbation; also, autoerotic practices favored over coitus.

Inverted: Orgasmic joy; felicitous sex relations; genital feasting; also, there is a possibility of happiness through sensual company perhaps via troilism or bisexuality; hedonism; Dionysian escapades; copious seminal discharges.

SEVEN

Auguries: Vivid sexual imagination; fantasies of extortionate orgasms and hypersexual partners; visions of subjugated phalli, male or female; fantasies of prolific penises and vaginas; superhuman sexual properties ascribed to mere humans; dreams of sexual mastery; also, sexual knowledge obtained through contemplation of sexual organs, copulation, and their meaning; also, past visions of sexual joy have not brought peace but the future holds deep and beautiful sexual experiences.

Inverted: Visionary sexuality will not come to pass; excessive masturbation leads to failure in healthy sexual relationships; vital passion spilled through masturbatory overindulgence; wasted orgasm; weak ejaculation; poor climax; also, impotence due to undermining thoughts of evil and violent sexual practices.

SIX

Auguries: The past and memories of sexual joy; recollections of copulations gone by; looking back upon virulent erections and violent orgasms; sexual nostalgia; preoccupation with thoughts of younger, sweeter sexual playmates; sexual happiness and sensual enjoyment, but coming from the past; lovers that have vanished; also, this card may represent lewd love letters from the past or mementos of days gone by, such as panties in the case of a lingerie fetishist.

Inverted: Copulation presently coming to pass; renewal of passionate endeavor; desire to change sexual partners and to create a new vibrant sex life; new sexual horizons; future ecstasy.

FIVE

Auguries: Partial sexual loss; some sexual partners no longer available; temporary impotence; sexual playmates growing away; also, a card of promising future sexual conquests but not corresponding to expectations; also, bitter sexual relationships; frustrated desires; marriage with troubles.

Inverted: Amatory news; promising sexual alliances; transmission of passion; sexual affinity; incestuous relations; return to virility.

FOUR

Auguries: Sexual weariness; disgust with copulating organs; imaginary sexual vexations; sexual discontent;

sexual satiety; boredom with orgasms; sex for sex's sake wearies one; disgust with demanding sexual desire; impatience with voracious sexual partners and rapacious genitals; bitter coital experiences; also, desire to find new sexual happiness, refreshing sexual experiences, and titillating sex mates.

Inverted: New sexual relations; exploratory sex; sexual initiation, perhaps into perversion; new erotic instruction; sexual novelty; also excesses and fatigue; bad health due to overindulgence in drinking, partying, and copulating.

THREE

Auguries: Extreme pleasure of the senses; sexual plenty; orgasmic fulfillment; sensual solace; victory over obstacles to sexual joy and victory over reluctant sex mates; sexual intercourse concluded in powerful orgasm; therapeutic climaxes; effulgent vaginas; adamantine penises; sexual gaiety; happiness; over-abundance; all will end well; orgasmic harvest; sexual comfort; speedy copulations.

Inverted: Sexual excess; rut; estrus; hypersexuality; intoxication; depravity; riotous sexual practices; unnatural lusts; insatiableness; sex for the sake of orgasm and self-pleasure; also, corollary impotence, delays, onanism, loss of virility.

TWO

Auguries: Copulation; passion; love; sexual union; concordant orgasms; vaginal penetration; anal intercourse; mutual masturbation; tribadism; interrelation of the sexes; mutual oral-genital practice; freedom in sex; sexual togetherness; like sexual sympathies; lasting sexual friendship.

Inverted: Separation of genitals; male divorced from female; a husband or wife unfaithful; the end of sexual union between two lovers; promises of orgasm broken; also, a friend will turn against the Querent; penis and vagina parted; unkept promises of sexual bliss; pretense of sensuousness; a penis of promising physical proportions is deceptive and cannot deliver supposed satisfaction; likewise, a flirtatious vagina is frigid.

ACE ♣ CUPS.

ACE

Auguries: Ultimate sexuality; fertility of sexual companionships; sensual joy; orgasmic nourishment; also, this card predicts a glorious mating of two lovers and a bountiful harvest of orgasms for both; fruitful coition; ecstasy.

Inverted: Sexual instability; asexuality; sterility; frigidity; unwilling sex partners; refused coition; loss of desire; sexual inertia; suspended sexual animation; penile flaccidity; *vaginismus.*

KING of WANDS

The Suit of Wands

KING

Auguries: A dark man, handsome, well-built, and the possessor of an overactive phallus; a physically minded man; an emotional man; an honest and friendly man; also, a man who understands the needs of others; also, honesty; news concerning an unexpected sexual affair.

Inverted: Good orgasms but via violent sex; strict sexual partners; also a man of high sexual principles; a severe man, often ruthless in bed; also, a man foolishly tolerant of sexual playmates who will do him more harm than good; a likely victim for sexual extortion.

QUEEN

Auguries: A dark woman, friendly, loving, but also exotic, sensual, and magnetic of personality; if the card beside her signifies a man, she is impassioned by him; a beautiful woman after whom men chase, but she is faithful and confines her sexual activities to one man

QUEEN of WANDS.   KNIGHT of WANDS.

at a time; a woman of great charm, devoted to servicing the phallus of her choice; also, dark sexuality; a loving paramour.

Inverted: A jealous woman; a woman of unstable emotions; deceitful woman; unfaithful lover; also, sexual opposition; infidelity; lying; also, a woman not to be trusted; a friendly but deceptive woman; a husband-stealer; a home-wrecker; if married, she is a woman who at the slightest hint of sexual coolness from her husband will take a lover.

KNIGHT

Auguries: A dark young man, attractive to women; a young man who "hits and runs" but never "kisses and tells"; also, hurried copulation, quick orgasm, speedy erection; sudden flight from one bed to another; departure from socially acceptable sexuality; change of sex partners; temporary coital abstinence; also, change of residence or sexual tastes.

Inverted: Onanism; partial orgasm; rupture; genital

separation; sexual quarreling; breaking up of a sexual alliance; also, an impetuous youth with an equally impetuous phallus.

PAGE

Auguries: A dark youth; a possible lover; also a young messenger or mailman who either brings news of a lover or is himself a likely sexual candidate; if followed by the Page of Cups, a dangerous rival phallus; also, a young heartbreaker who has nothing for women but a stiff sex organ; a youthful gigolo; a secret love.

Inverted: Indecisive lover; reluctant phallus; emotional instability; *coitus interruptus;* also, a young lover who tells all; a sexual gossip; also, bad news concerning desired orgasms.

PAGE of WANDS.

Auguries: Satiety; guilt over evil sexual practices; the burden of satisfying many sex partners; the burden of too many orgasms; pregnancy worries; fear of discovery by cuckolded husbands; sexual oppression; also, venereal disease as a result of sexual greed.

Inverted: An unfaithful lover, a liar; one who causes pregnancies and disappears; one who breaks promises; a false penis; a lover who promises orgasm but achieves only his own; also, sexual success is restricted if the Nine of Swords follows; in a paternal lawsuit, there will be certain loss.

NINE

Auguries: Strength of phallus in opposition of phalli; hidden penile enemies near; strength to overcome sexual opposition is within the Querent; fearless passion; inflamed lust met with inflamed lust; equal passion; also, formidable orgasms; nymphomaniacal insatiety equalled by satyrical desire.

Inverted: Obstacles to orgasm; sexual adversity; suspension of desire; orgies delayed; paternity worries; bad luck with love objects; sexual competition weighty; calamity in love; also, opposing phalli predominate.

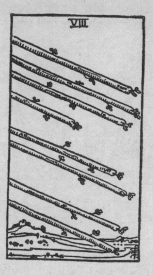

EIGHT

Auguries: Arrows of love; activity in sexual undertakings; the path of sexual activity; also, copulative motion; changed sexual taste or sex mates changed; hurried orgasms; swift coition; great hope of phallic conquest; speed towards orgiastic climax; moving penis; vibrant clitoris; also, sexual decisions made hurriedly.

Inverted: Arrows of jealousy; quick reaching out for orgasm without thought of the sex partner; fights over who possesses the love object; in cases of troilism and orgies, quarreling over who shall do what to whom and when; for couples, disputes over orgasmic achievements; also, guilty conscience.

SEVEN

Auguries: Many sexual enemies or competitors; advantage over these; the idomitable phallus is victorious over all others; success for the sexually aggressive; superior sexuality challenged; love-fights; success in sexual jousts; mastery over attacking phalli; sexual prowess.

Inverted: Sexual embarrassments; perplexing sexual demands; also, hesitancy in copulation will bring about great loss; anxiety; distress; impotence; also, a caution against erotic indecision.

SIX

Auguries: Promising news of great orgasms; victorious coitus; triumphant climaxes; copulation crowned with its own desire; the crown of sexual mastery; sexual gratification follows patient waiting; sexual supremacy.

Inverted: Apprehensive sensuality; fear, as of a victorious penis at the entrance to a lover's vagina; vague fears cloud optimistic coition; treacherous lover; vagina opened to the enemy; disloyalty; phallus (penis or clitoris) erecting for competitors; also, jealousy may lead to discord between rival phalli.

FIVE

Auguries: Games of sexual pursuit lead to misery; worthless fighting, as over possession of penis or vagina; imitation love; spurious desire; also, violent competition for orgasmic riches; the battle of sex after sex; also, unquenchable lust; the lusts of many for the favors of one; lusting leads to failure; this is the card of the lover who will not quit while he is ahead and who will in time lose the sources of orgasm now at his disposal.

Inverted: A cheating sex mate; sexual trickery; vitality sapped by quarrels; contradictory demands from the sex partner; loss of virility through the deceit of a lover.

FOUR

Auguries: Orgasmic security; haven of sexuality; a houseful of lovers; sexual concord; genital harmony; prosperous affairs; a bounty of orgasms; also, embellished phallus; beautiful genitals; increased love juices; lovely sexual organs.

Inverted: Masturbation; loss of paramours; flaccid phalli and unresponsive clitorises; everything gone for those who have made sex the foundation of their life; autoerotism; autoerotic practices.

THREE

Auguries: Sexual discovery; established duration of copulation; orgasmic effort; sexual mastery; abundant semen for multiple coitus; also, sexual help will come in time of frustration; a man of passion will copulate and end problems of passivity or frigidity.

Inverted: Spilled semen; wasted orgasms; unfulfilled climaxes; masturbation; rejection by desired phalli; sexual outcast; in time of great sexual need, one will try to lure you to perversion.

TWO

Auguries: Erotic fantasies realized; sexual riches; virile genitals; beautiful phalli; orgiastic bliss; a fortune of orgasms; victorious copulations; sated desires; abundant penile ejaculations; prolific vaginal excretions; also, lust and sex rather than love and marriage; a passionate woman will be asked to copulate with a wealthy man; a man with a large phallus will come into the Querent's life.

Inverted: Sex acts devoid of excitement; loss of faith in genitally-produced happiness; passion cooled; lack of lust; desires thwarted; also, the Dionysian spirit will be denied, causing unhappiness despite frequent copulations.

ACE of WANDS.

ACE

Auguries: Virility; fertility; sexual creativity; many orgasms; playful sexual inventions; enterprising sexuality; the starting point of sexual escapades; playful phalli; birth of new coital partners; beginning of exciting sexual alliances; childlike sensuality; original sexual diversions to please the senses.

Inverted: Masturbation; venereal disease; castration, perhaps circumcision; void wombs; empty vaginas; weak phalli; impotence; frigidity; sexual stupor; insensitiveness.

KING of SWORDS.

The Suit
of Swords

KING

Auguries: Sexual potency; command of robust orgasms; peerless phalli; incomparable sexual technique; unparalleled passion; erotic power; militant sexuality; also, a man possessing these; a man who will take command of sexual pursuits; sexual authority; hypersensuality.

Inverted: A brilliant but sadistic man; one who would plan the overthrow of a happy sexual relationship; a sadist; also, cruelty; perversity; sexual aberrations; barbarous sex acts; evil intention; also, this is the card of sadists and flagellants.

QUEEN

Auguries: Disunion; solitude; female sadness; insensitiveness; frigidity; in a sense, lesbianism; sterility; embarrassment; separation from sexual joy; phallic privation; masturbation due to aloneness; also, mourning over a lost lover; painful desire for past phalli.

101

Inverted: Treacherous female deceitful vagina; bigoted love; sexual malice; artificial sensuality; also, prudishness; bigotry; suppressed desires; false virginity; false chastity.

QUEEN of SWORDS.   KNIGHT of SWORDS.

KNIGHT

Auguries: A forceful man; a cold and efficient man whose depth of emotion manifests itself only in the sexual embrace; a man who conquers the sexual objects of his choice; also, sexual skill; bravery in the face of opposition; great orgasmic capacity; passion; sexual determination; fearless coition; dedicated libertinism.

Inverted: Sexual troubles; impulsive sex; erotic imprudence; lack of finesse; unskillful copulation; awkward phalli; also, a young man representing these; an extravagant young man who spends entirely too much money for sex he can enjoy through other means; an impulsive young man who "goes too fast."

PAGE of SWORDS.

PAGE

Auguries: A voyeur; a young man who masturbates when viewing erotic photographs or literature; a peeping Tom; a sexually curious young man or woman; youngsters who enjoy viewing the passion and coitus of others; oglers; also, vigilance, in the sense of assuring one's privacy while secretly viewing the phalli of others; also, a youthful lover who, because of age, secretly indulges in sex acts.

Inverted: Sickness; depression; sexual inadequacy; premature copulation; also, the more evil side of the above auguries; unforeseen results to early sexual indulgence; weakened sexuality through misuse; unprepared phalli.

TEN

Auguries: Genital pain; venereal disease; hypersensitive phalli; nymphomania; satyriasis; insatiableness; phallic affliction; desires unquenched; also, depressing solitude; ungratifying autoerotism; unsatisfying masturbation; tears of loneliness; flaccid phalli; miseries of un-requited passion and desire.

Inverted: Sexual authority: orgasmic profit; sexual successes; erotic power; favor in the eyes of desired sex mates; but none of these are permanent.

NINE

Auguries: Sad news, as of a sexual partner who has died, is sexually cheating, has other lovers, or has contracted venereal disease; also utter desolation; castration; celibacy; pregnancy when not desired; miscarriage; sexual shame; disgrace; orgasmic delays; disappointing phalli; coital failure; inefficient copulation; false phalli.

Inverted: A broken hymen; a young girl will lose her virginity; also, a sexual relationship broken by another man or woman; reasonable fear of venereal disease; doubt about sex partner's genitals; suspicious lover; sexual shame due to diseased sexual organs; confined genitals, medically speaking.

EIGHT

Auguries: Sexual slavery; temporary confinement; forced patterns of sexuality; sexual cruelty; domination by a person sexually perverted; abuse of sexual organs; flagellation; sadism; white slavery; sexual extortion; also, a sexual crisis; conflict of morals and desires; bad news concerning one's sexual propensities; also, sickness; venereal disease.

Inverted: Laborious copulation; sexual disquiet; unruly genitalia; hypersensitive penis or clitoris; difficulty with an overactive libido; opposition between lust and morality; also, terror of unknown phalli; treacherous hungers; unforeseen orgasms.

SEVEN

Auguries: Lewd designs; concupiscent wishes; hope of orgasm; sexual confidence; faith in one's amatory technique; reliable phalli; also, the card predicts sexual fantasies realized; new phalli; new sexual partners; wealth of penile (clitoral) erections followed by new and confidence-building orgasms.

105

Inverted: Quarrels over orgasms that have failed; arguments about sexuality; displeasure with phalli; phallic faultfinding; babbling and slander connected with one's sexual technique.

SIX

Auguries: Sensuous journey upon the fluids of Bartholin glands; prolific seminal discharges; the fluidity of casual intercourse; sex mates easily acquired; an affluence of orgasms; also, the Querent will meet a new sex mate while on a trip or journey; also, expedient copulation.

Inverted: Be prepared for an unexpected proposal of sexual union. This may come from a homosexual or lesbian or from a neighbor least likely to fornicate; also, sexual confessions or confessions of secret lust; in a lesser sense, beware of public disclosure.

FIVE

Auguries: Degrading sexuality; penis destruction; *vaginismus;* dishonor; sexual loss, either of potency or of sexual playmates; sexual deviation; also, rape or multiple copulation; also, conquering phalli; warning to be considerate of those sexually unfortunate or those who are less beautifully endowed phallically.

Inverted: Death of sex; castration; frigidity; impotence; also, phalli falling into disuse; necrophiliac tendencies; funereal erotism; sexual excitation at a funeral; also, meeting sexual partners at a funeral.

FOUR

Auguries: Sexual retreat; solitude; inactive phalli; tranquility of lustful desires; peace in the face of turbulent sexuality; sensual repose; also, the card of religious bigots who endeavor to deny sexuality; self-exile from passion; masturbatory practices perpetrated secretly; temporary seclusion for sexual reflection.

Inverted: Suspended use of genitals; economical copulation; wise methods of coitus; vigilant phalli; cautious coition; temporary self-imposed celibacy for recuperative reasons.

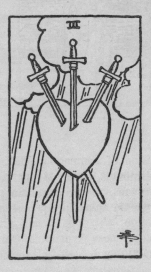

THREE

Auguries: The meaning of the design is implicit: Heartbreak; rupture in sexual companionship; phallicism denied; copulation refused; orgasmic delay; absence of willing genitials; upheaval in the sexual life; removal of a cherished source of passion and orgasm.

Inverted: Sexual incompatibility; copulative errors; loss of potency or lack of erections; sexual disorder; confusion of sexual interests; strife in the erotic bed.

TWO

Auguries: Fusion of compatible phalli; sexual balance; coital harmony; tender loving relations with erectile sexual organs; tender copulation; affectionate embraces and gentle copulation; phallic friendship; sexual concord.

Inverted: Masochistic tendencies at work; danger of impending sexual cruelty; sexual impostors; lying to dominate sexually; unfaithful phalli; bisexuality; sexual duplicity; disloyal sex mates.

ACE

Auguries: Triumphant penis or clitoris; sexual success; conquest of obstacles, such as the love object's inhibitions, reservations, and clothes; triumphant of the erected phallus over hesitant sex mates; also, it is a card of great force in hatred as well as in love; strong emotions; winning sexual ways; orgasm the crown of penile dexterity.

Inverted: The same as above but with disastrous results; pregnancy; violent sex; torn hymens; bruised phalli; sexual anomalies; misused sexual organs; also, childbirth.

ACE of SWORDS.

KING ◊ PENTACLES.

The Suit
of Pentacles

KING

Auguries: A virile dark man; an affectionate mate; an intelligent man who can reason his way into any bed; also, sexual bravery; aptitude for surmounting obstacles to orgasm; sexual successes; monetary gifts bring genital gifts in return.

Inverted: Bribery for orgasm; vice; purchased sexual favors; misuse of money for orgasmic gain; sexual and monetary extravagance; drunkenness and orgiastic sexuality; corruption of youth; sexual perversion; perilous sexual activities; epicurism; gluttony; also, sexual weakness; ugly or unclean phalli.

QUEEN

Auguries: Orgasmic opulence phallic generosity; sexual freedom; sex for sex's sake; also, a woman manifesting these; a woman of magnificent beauty; beauty of the phallus; generous copulations; fruitful coitus; wealth of sensual pleasures; exciting sexual escapades; titilated phalli; piqued erogenous zones; also, a woman who worships the male phallus.

Inverted: A sexually cruel woman, sadistic in the bed of love; a fellatrix; a vicious, licentious woman; an unsated woman who lives in a constant state of sexual anxiety; also, mistrust of sexual partners; evil sex; fearful erotic fantasies; relationships without trust; suspicious passion and desires.

QUEEN of PENTACLES

KNIGHT of PENTACLES

KNIGHT

Auguries: A young man, qualified to teach sexual techniques; a young sensualist; a young man who will buy a woman's love, not with money but by providing her with numerous gratifying orgasms; also, sexual service; utility of phalli; orgasmic responsibility; surroundings of beauty; the good things of life; sexual achievement and orgasmic plenty.

Inverted: Narrowmindedness; sexual inertia; stagnant sexual technique; impotent copulations; idle masturbation; careless coition; preoccupation with personal orgasms; inability to yield; one-track mindedness; confined to desultory sex acts; discouragement of exploratory sex and sexual positions.

PAGE

Auguries: A young man or boy who applies himself studiously to variations of the sex act; a young lover; a catamite; a young daydreamer who may be cultivated by the right sex mate; also, sexual application; phallic study; thoughts of the sex acts and the sexual organs; sexual curiosity; the pubescent boy or girl.

Inverted: A rebellious youth, boy or girl; a youth of the "hippie" philosophy; a sensual but reckless youth; also, wasteful sex; lavish erections; nonconforming sex; extreme passion; reckless desires.

TEN

Auguries: Orgasmic gain; sensual riches; abundant copulations; acquisition of intense erotic pleasure; penile or clitoral erections galore.

Inverted: Loss of virginity; loss of potency; frigidity; loss of sensual pleasure with a sex mate; minimal orgasms; also, danger of rape; pursuit of the sexual favors of another man's wife is a gamble and will be lost; also, an illegitimate child; bastard sex; unholy phalli.

NINE

Auguries: Safety in penile possession; a youth whose lover is true; also, certain orgasm; fulfilled promises of sexual bliss; erotic successes; copulative accomplishments; sexual foresight; the accumulation of orgasms.

Inverted: Danger of stolen orgasms; orgasms artifically produced; stormy passion; sexual fruit destroyed; desecration of sexual union; deceiving lovers; onanism; wasted semen; abused phalli.

EIGHT

Auguries: Genital manipulation; skillful coition; copulations of art; industrious sexual labor; plodding passion; coital craftsmanship; dextrous phalli; also, the beginning of fruitful sexual relations; new sexual demands met; also, skill at sexual foreplay.

Inverted: Vain phalli; voided sexual ambitions; false promises of orgasm; phallic disillusionment; also, a person of vanity who boasts of magnificent or promising sexual organs but fails to deliver; the card of the transvestite.

SEVEN

Auguries: The card of the procurer or pimp; money talks; orgasms are purchased; also, the card of the proverbial dirty old man who pays young girls for sexual intercourse; also, barter; trading sex for something one wants; orgasms provided in return for social success; the prostitute's card.

Inverted: Impudent sexual activities; orgasms will not be mutual; unrequited passions and desires; foreplay does not result in seminal emission.

SIX

Auguries: The Querent will be looked upon favorably by a desired love object; sexual kindness; beneficent copulation; orgasms shared; the sexually underprivileged treated equally; a just phallus; also, this is the card of interracial sex; phallics for one and all; nondiscriminating coitus.

Inverted: Raw lust; passionate desire; lewdness; depravity; jealousy over sex partners; illusory fears about superior phalli; evil deeds; sadism; sexual torture.

FIVE

Auguries: Sexual destitution; loss of wife, husband, lover, or mistress; absence of contraception at the point of dire need; undesired pregnancy; hysterectomy; circumcision; castration; also, rejection by family, friends, cohorts, or sexual playmates.

FOUR

Auguries: The surety of status quo; clinging to sex partners which one now has; enjoyment of present methods of orgasm; certain copulation.

Inverted: Sexual opposition in the offing; guard one's genitals or virginity or chastity; genitalia in danger; sexual suspense; threatening evildoers, such as rapists, perverts, pederasts, etc.

THREE

Auguries: Orgasms received through artistic love-making; the Querent, or someone in the Querent's life, is highly skilled in the art of love; sexual renown; orgasmic glory; skillful copulation; lithe phalli; manipulative genitals; capable sexual techniques; glorious climaxes; sex mates obtained through reputation.

Inverted: Mediocre coitus; ineffective phalli; insipid passion; sexual daydreams undermine sexual creativity; debilitating masturbation; liquefied semen; petty desires.

TWO

Auguries: Celebrations, parties; orgies; much gaiety; carefree sex relations; intersexual relations; genital recreation; exploratory sexual activities for fun; laughter and music and wine and dancing; playful seductive girls; sensuous boys and men; strip poker; troilism; swinging; happy orgasms.

Inverted: False gaiety; drunkenness leading to impotence; intoxications sap passion and desire; outward fun, inward misery; excessive sexual intercourse but minimal orgasms; simulated success and satiation.

Auguries: Money in the bank; superior phalli; excellent genitals; sexual contentment; ecstasy; sensual bliss; speedy orgasms; fruitful coitions; happiness with all sex mates; full understanding of the beauty of sex and the phallus; enduring erections; lasting orgasms; pleasant passion.

Inverted: Money used for evil purposes; paid intercourse; prostitution; evil sex; sexual greed; extortionate desires; jealousy; envy of other phalli; ill-gotten sexual slaves; the young corrupted by money; young girls paid to commit perverse sex acts; young boys corrupted sexually with money.

Part Three

HOW TO MAKE
A SPREAD

How to Make a Spread

The Dealer first selects a card to represent the matter or person in question. This card is called the Agent. Place the Agent on a table, face upwards, and shuffle and cut the rest of the pack three times.

Taking the top card of the shuffled and cut deck, cover the Agent with it. This card represents the person's or the matter's general atmosphere and it symbolizes the influence presently surrounding the Agent.

Next, take the second card from the deck. Lay it across the first. This is the Obstacle Card and it crosses the Agent, symbolizing the obstacles in the matter at hand.

Take up the third card and place it above the Agent. This is the Crown card and represents the best that can be expected under the circumstances.

The fourth card is the Foundation Card and is placed below the Agent. It shows what has already passed and what the Agent identifies with.

The fifth card is the Past Card and should be placed behind the Agent, that is, away from where he is looking. This card represents a past influence or an influence or influences now passing.

NOTE: If the Agent Card cannot be said to face either way, the Dealer should determine beforehand which way it is facing.

Taking up the sixth card, place it before the Agent. This is the future Card and it depicts the influence which will come into operation shortly.

The cards now form a cross. The Agent is in the center, covered by his Atmosphere Card. Now the next four cards are turned up. Place them to the right of the cross, one after the other, so the tenth card is uppermost.

To enumerate, the seventh card is the Attitude Card and signifies the Agent and his position in the present situation. The eighth is the House Card and represents the influence of the Agent's immediate family and friends. The ninth card represents the Agent's hopes or fears in the matter being considered. And the tenth card is the Culmination Card and it means what will come. It represents the final result of the combined influences of the other cards.

In this type of spread it is possible to ask particular questions, the answers alluded to by the tenth card. Or, if desired, the cross spread can be used for a life reading, divination of a person's present condition.

The Tarot can do only so much. It is wise to remember that much depends upon the Reader's or Dealer's intuition. The greater a Reader's intuitive faculties, the better the reading.

Part Four

CHOOSING AN AGENT

Choosing an Agent

Choosing the Agent is the most important step in divination by cards. There are many ways of accomplishing this. There is the concept at large which suggests that the Court Cards (Kings, Queens, Knights, Pages) of the four suits correspond to various classifications of people. It comes out thus:

PENTACLES—Swarthy complexion, dark brown or black hair, dark eyes.

WANDS—Fair complexion, blond or auburn hair, blue eyes.

SWORDS—Dull complextion, dark brown hair, grey or hazel eyes

CUPS—Fair complexion, dull fair hair or light brown hair, grey or blue eyes.

The above method may be used but we argue the validity of the procedure in that the color of one's skin, eyes, or hair, rarely influences ones sexuality. Therefore, for our purposes, a more exacting method of choosing an Agent must be devised. In concert with the mystics of old, we maintain that a person's sexuality is as close as his very act of respiration. Therefore we turn our attention to other sources of identification.

It has been noted in the commentary on the Magician Card at the beginning of this book that the four suits of the Tarot correspond to the four elements; that is, Wands and Fire, Cups and Water, Swords and Earth, Pentacles and Air. It is from this ancient mystical truth that a method for choosing an Agent arises.

To begin, the Agent's age and birthdate should be determined. A Queen should be chosen as the Agent for a woman who is over forty years of age; and a Page for any female less than forty. If the subject is a man over forty, a Knight should be chosen as Agent; and a King should represent a man under forty.

Now to the suits. If the Agent was born between March 21 and April 20 or July 23 and August 22 or November 22 and December 22, the suit is Wands, corresponding to Fire, the sign of Aries, Leo, and Sagittarius.

If the Agent was born between April 21 and May 22 or August 23 and September 22 or December 23 and January 20, the suit is Swords, corresponding to Earth, the sign of Taurus, Virgo and Capricorn.

If the Agent was born between May 23 and June 21 or September 23 and October 22 or January 21 and February 19, the suit is Pentacles, corresponding to Air, the sign of Gemini, Libra, and Aquarius.

If the Agent was born between June 22 and July 22 or October 23 and November 21 or February 20 and March 20, the suit is Cups, corresponding to Water, the sign of Cancer, Scorpio, and Pisces.

As an example: A woman, thirty-six years of age, born on the tenth of August would be represented by the Page of Wands.

With the Agent chosen properly, the ensuing cards of the spread will be more meaningful, informative, and revealing.